Hodder Gibson

Scottish Examination Materi

HIGHER

GERMAN

Practice Papers

Reading and Directed Writing

Calum E. Ure, M.A. Hons

Hodder Gibson

A MEMBER OF THE HODDER HEADLINE GROUP

P.K

INTRODUCTION

This book is intended to help candidates prepare for the 80-hour unit of the Higher Still German examination. The material presented in this book gives candidates much needed practice in some of the tasks set at Higher level. I hope too that teachers and college lecturers will find this book a good source of relevant, topical and interesting materials to complement the Higher Still course.

Some of the Reading passages in this book appeared in the first edition of *Higher German Practice Papers*. The texts, however, have since been shortened, modified and simplified to be an accurate reflection of what candidates can expect in the new Higher Still examination. The questions have been completely revised in keeping with the style of the new exam.

The book is divided into six parts: Reading Tests for preparation for the final exam, Answer Schemes, Directed Writing tasks, Phrases to help candidates prepare for Directed Writing, Reading Tests to prepare for the end of unit tests and Answer Schemes.

ACKNOWLEDGEMENTS

My grateful thanks to Silke Schatz for her suggested translations, Kenneth McLaren for his English proof-reading skills and especially to the pupils of St Columba's School, Kilmacolm, for trying out all the material.

Every effort has been made to trace copyright holders of material produced in this book. Any rights not acknowledged here will be acknowledged in subsequent printings if notice is given to the publishers.

Orders: please contact Bookpoint Ltd, 130 Milton Park, Abingdon, Oxon OX14 4SB. Telephone: (44) 01235 827720. Fax: (44) 01235 400454. Lines are open from 9.00 – 6.00, Monday to Saturday, with a 24 hour messag answering services. You can also order through our website www.hoddereducation.co.uk.

British Library Cataloguing in Publication Data
A catalogue record for this title is available from the British Library

ISBN-10: 0-340-81209-5
ISBN-13: 978-0-340-81209-9

Published by Hodder Gibson, 2a Christie Street, Paisley PA1 1NB.
Tel: 0141 848 1609; Fax: 0141 889 6315; email: hoddergibson@hodder.co.uk
First published 2003
Impression number   10 9 8 7 6 5 4 3 2
Year   2008 2007 2006 2005

Typeset by Fakenham Photosetting Limited, Fakenham, Norfolk
Printed and bound in Great Britain by Martins The Printers, Berwick-upon-Tweed for Hodder Gibson, 2a Christie Street, Paisley, PA1 1NB, Scotland, UK

CONTENTS

READING

DIRECTED WRITING

END OF UNIT READING TESTS

RECORD OF ACHIEVEMENT

ADVICE TO TEACHERS

READING

The texts in this book are all taken from authentic German material. They are presented under three themes: *Lifestyles*, *Education and Work* and *The Wider World*. The texts are set alphabetically, not in order of difficulty. Each of the practice texts for the External Assessment paper has a section underlined for translation. I have provided a glossary after each text in which I have tried to include any words which do not appear in either the *Collins Pocket German*, the *Heinemann Harrap German School* or the *Collins German plus Grammar* dictionaries.

Each of the texts relates directly to one of the three themes, and I would suggest that candidates work through the section corresponding to the theme they are currently studying in class. In this way, the students will be familiar with that area of vocabulary, and the text will help to consolidate what they already know, as well as to broaden their knowledge on that subject. For candidates with less ability, a text directly related to the theme they are studying in class will be more readily accessible to them.

At the start of the academic year when students are faced with longer pieces of prose for the first time, you may choose to work through a relevant text with the candidates. As the year goes on and candidates become more confident, you may decide that they can work more independently on the texts and correct their own work using the Answer Schemes provided. By the end of the academic year candidates should be able to tackle any of the texts on their own and feel a sense of achievement in their own accomplishment. (They can monitor their own progress by keeping a record of their marks in the Record of Achievement section at the back of this book.)

At stages during the year, you may decide to set a text under exam conditions to see how well the candidates perform in the time given.

SPEAKING

Each of the texts can be exploited for speaking practice. As they all relate to the Higher Still themes, they can all be used as a stimulus for either group or class discussion. More able candidates can be asked to read a certain passage and can then be asked questions in German about the text to check their comprehension and initiate discussion.

DIRECTED WRITING AND DIRECTED WRITING PHRASES

All the Directed Writing topics require candidates to write predominantly in the past tense and to use future or conditional tenses too. I have included some phrases intended for those candidates who are working without the constant help of a classroom teacher or lecturer. The phrases are divided up under headings and relate to a certain bullet point in the Directed Writing topics. Of course, candidates should be encouraged to use their own ideas and language, but if they do refer to the Directed Writing Phrases section, they should be encouraged to learn each new phrase so that it becomes part of their own language and can be successfully incorporated into another Directed Writing task at a later date.

As with the Reading texts, at appropriate stages during the year you may decide to set one of the Directed Writing topics as a forty-minute test and impose exam conditions on the candidates.

END OF UNIT READING TESTS

I have included nine Reading tests relating to the three themes of *Lifestyles*, *Education and Work* and *The Wider World*. These passages are shorter than the others, include more questions and do not contain a translation section. You may wish to set candidates one of these prior to the end of unit test for extra practice. (As these Practice Papers are widely available and Answer Schemes are provided, these tests will <u>not</u> be accepted as evidence that candidates have gained the unit award.)

ANSWER SCHEMES

I provide answers to all of the questions and suggested translations. So that the candidates do not feel disadvantaged, I have referred to the *Collins Pocket German*, the *Heinemann Harrap German School* and the *Collins German Plus Grammar* dictionaries, and where appropriate I have used their suggested translations in the first instance.

READING

ADVICE TO CANDIDATES

- Read the title and the English introduction.
- Read the text thoroughly before you begin, referring to the glossary at the end of the passage.
- Read through all the questions before you start, as they reveal much about the text.
- Read through the text a second time, looking up any words in the dictionary which impede your comprehension.
- Remember that the information required for each answer falls in order. The answer to question 1 will be at the start of the text, the next answer will come after that, etc.
- Read through all the questions in one group before starting to write your answers, e.g. 2 *(a)*, *(b)* and *(c)*. As the answers will all be in one section of the text, make sure your answers correspond directly to the correct questions.
- A question worth 2 points requires two separate pieces of information, a question worth 3 points requires three separate pieces of information, etc.
- Do not be tempted to translate every word literally. Try to paraphrase without omitting any of the essential information.
- Read through your answer before moving on to the next question. Does it make perfect sense in English? Have you included enough information for the number of points?
- Although it may take you longer at the start of the Higher year, practise answering all the questions (and translation section) in one hour.
- Take a note of any new words or phrases which appeal to you and learn them. The wider your vocabulary, the better you will perform in the Reading (and the other papers in the Higher Still examination).
- If you are having difficulty with one question, move on to the next and come back to it at the end.

TRANSLATION

ADVICE TO CANDIDATES

- Read the underlined section carefully and try to make sense of it before starting to write.
- Read what comes before and after the translation section so that you can put the section into context.
- In translating each word literally, it may not sound English or it may be rather stilted. Try to remain faithful to the sense of the German and convey this naturally in English.
- Identify all the verbs and recognise the correct tense.
- Identify all plural nouns, e.g. *Flohmärkte*, *Stapel*, *Dosen*, *Vorstellungsgespräche*, etc., and make sure you make them plural in English.
- Think carefully about what to look up in the dictionary. For example: *Blutlachen*. This is a compound word, i.e. a word that is formed from joining two (or more) other words. In this instance you need to look up *Blut* – which gives you 'blood' – and *Lache* – which gives you 'pool'. Note that *Lache* here is plural – *Lachen*. If you put the meaning of both words together, *Blutlachen* can be translated as 'pools of blood'.

THE MARKING OF THE READING AND TRANSLATION

The comprehension questions are worth 20 marks and the translation is worth 10 marks.

In your answers in the Reading it is important that you show your comprehension of the text and that you can convey this factual information with as much detail and accuracy as possible. The number of points for each question corresponds to the number of points you have to write down from the text. On occasion, certain questions may be worth less than the number of points you can take from the text, e.g. a question may be worth 3 points but there may be 5 separate pieces of information in the text, each worth 1 point.

Each of the translation sections is divided into 5 'sense units'. Two possible marks are awarded to each unit. If your translation of a unit is 'good', you will be awarded 2 marks. If your translation is 'satisfactory', you will be given 1 mark. No marks are awarded for an 'unsatisfactory' translation. In simple terms, if you fail to demonstate sufficient understanding or you mistranslate, you gain no marks. If your translation conveys your comprehension but is imprecise, you will be awarded 1 mark. If your translation is precise and is conveyed clearly, you will receive 2 marks for that 'sense unit'.

READING

LIFESTYLES

Passage 1

Read this magazine article carefully, then answer **in English** the questions which follow it. You may use a German dictionary.

This article is about the reaction of a 10-year-old girl to her parents' separation.

Der Tag, an dem Papa fortging

Es ist windig und die Zweige[1] kratzen an der Fensterscheibe. Maren wacht auf. Sie friert. An schrecklichen Tagen, das weiß sie, friert man immer. Und heute war ein schrecklicher Tag gewesen. Heute war Papa fortgegangen.

5 „Vielleicht habe ich das alles ja nur geträumt" denkt sie, „manchmal träumt man etwas und glaubt, es ist wirklich passiert." Aber im Licht der Straßenlaterne sieht sie den Zettel auf dem Nachttisch und weiß, dass es kein Traum war. Auf dem Zettel steht Onkel Friedrichs Adresse. Da könne sie ihn immer erreichen, hatte ihr Vater gesagt, sie könne auch anrufen, zu jeder Zeit.

10 Sie stand am Garagentor und sah zu, wie ihr Vater seine Sachen ins Auto packte. Das große Bild mit dem Schiff darauf nahm er auch mit. Mit so einem Schiff wollten sie um die Welt fahren. Und jetzt? „Das machen wir trotzdem", sagte er, „versprochen!" Und dann war er weggefahren. Wie jeden Morgen, als ob er in ein paar Stunden zurückkäme. Bevor er ins Auto

15 gestiegen war, hatte er sie fest in den Arm genommen. Sein Gesicht war nass, so wie im letzten Jahr, als der Großvater gestorben war, und er versprach, bald wiederzukommen. Nicht für immer, das nicht, aber zu Besuch. Wann? Erst müsse er verreisen, aber in drei Wochen ganz bestimmt. Und dann jeden zweiten Sonntag. Sie würden tolle Sachen

20 machen, Oma Meier besuchen und endlich nach Legoland fahren. Und in den Ferien zusammen nach Eurodisney, sie beide ganz allein, das wäre doch schön?

Das mit den drei Wochen hatte sich Maren vorm Schlafengehen noch in ihren Schülerkalender geschrieben. Denn manchmal vergessen

25 Erwachsene leider, was sie versprochen haben.

Morgens beim Frühstück hatte sie es gleich gemerkt. Mama hatte dicke
Augen, und Papa tat zweimal Zucker in den Tee. Maren war noch müde.
Sie hatte schlecht geschlafen, weil es im Wohnzimmer wieder laut gewesen
war. „Brüll[2] nicht so", hatte ihre Mutter irgendwann geschrien, „du weckst
30 das Kind auf!" Aber da war Maren schon wach gewesen. Sie wäre gern
hinunter ins Wohnzimmer gegangen, aber sie hatte sich nicht getraut[3].
Wenn es in den letzten Monaten Krach gab, tat sie immer so, als ob sie
schlafe. Sonst würden sie nur wieder erzählen, dass alles nur Spaß wäre,
oder sie antworteten ihr ewiges „Ach Kind, das verstehst du noch nicht "
35 und hatten nach den Schulaufgaben gefragt oder ob sie schon aufgeräumt
habe. Nie gab es Antworten. Und was sollte sie da glauben?

Maren überlegt, wann alles angefangen hatte. Ostern? Doch, von da an
hatte sich alles verändert. „Maren", sagte die Mutter und legte ihre Hand
auf Marens. „Papa und ich haben einen Entschluss gefasst[4]. Du musst keine
40 Angst haben . . . " Aber Maren hatte trotzdem Angst. „Ich werde ausziehen,
Kind", sagte der Vater schnell, „das hat aber gar nichts mit uns beiden zu
tun. Mama und ich wollen nicht mehr zusammenleben, aber du wirst mich
ganz oft besuchen, am Wochenende. Du bist ja schon zehn, so groß und
vernünftig . . ." Niemand sprach mehr. Ob sie sich jetzt scheiden lassen wollen? Die
45 Mutter nickte und ging schnell ins Bad. „Sag doch was, Kind", sagte der
Vater, aber ihr war nichts eingefallen.

Jetzt fällt ihr viel ein, aber jetzt ist er weg. Sie trennen sich, weil sie sich
nicht mehr lieb genug haben. Vielleicht geht er gar nicht wegen Mama.
Vielleicht geht er, weil sie, Maren, nicht lieb genug war . . .

50 Sie friert jetzt nicht mehr. Ihre Augen brennen, und trotzdem kann sie nicht
weinen. Sie will nach ihrer Mutter rufen, aber sie traut sich nicht. Sie will
sie nicht belästigen, damit nicht auch Mama weggehen muss. „Warum
haben sie mir dann immer erzählt, dass alles in Ordnung ist?" überlegt
Maren. Was waren denn die Tatsachen?

55 Leise öffnet sich ihre Zimmertür. „Kannst du auch nicht schlafen?" hört sie
ihre Mutter leise fragen. „Willst du heute nicht mal bei mir schlafen?
Ausnahmsweise[5]? Es ist doch eine so kalte Nacht . . ."

1   der Zweig (e): twig
2   brüllen: to yell
3   sich trauen: to dare
4   einen Entschluss fassen: to make a decision
5   ausnahmsweise: just this once

QUESTIONS

1. Maren's father has left, but Maren thinks she may just have dreamt this (lines 4–9).

   What proof is there that her father has gone for good?   **2 points**

2. In paragraph 3 Maren thinks back over the day's events and her father's departure (lines 10–22).

   (a)   Why was the big picture of the ship important to Maren?   **1 point**

   (b)   How do we know that her father was upset?   **1 point**

   (c)   When had Maren last seen her father in such a state?   **1 point**

   (d)   What outings did he promise to go on with his daughter?   **3 points**

3. It was at family breakfasts that Maren first realised that things were not working out between her parents (lines 26–36).

   (a)   What evidence was there that her parents had not slept well?   **2 points**

   (b)   Why had Maren not slept well again?   **1 point**

   (c)   Maren's parents were not honest. How did they respond to her questions?   **3 points**

4. Maren thinks back to the time her parents told her they were splitting up (lines 37–46). How did her father try to reassure her?   **2 points**

5. We are given an insight into Maren's reaction to their separation (lines 47–54).

   (a)   What conclusions does she draw?   **2 points**

   (b)   Why does she not want to call out to her mother?   **2 points**

        (20 points)

        = 20 marks

6. Translate into English:

   „Das machen wir trotzdem … fest in den Arm genommen." (lines 12–15)   **10**

        (30)

Passage 2

Read this magazine article carefully, then answer **in English** the questions which follow it. You may use a German dictionary.

This article is about young people from a small, provincial German town and how they spend their free time.

Ein Wochenende in der Provinz

Anklam liegt 170 Kilometer nördlich von Berlin. Die Kleinstadt hat 18.000 Einwohner, eine Hauptstraße und 642 Jugendliche zwischen 15 und 17, von denen jeder jeden kennt. In Anklam gibt es so gut wie keine Freizeitangebote für junge Leute. Der einzige Jugendclub der Stadt hat nur
5   dienstags und donnerstags ein paar Stunden geöffnet. Ins städtische Mini-Schwimmbad gehen nur Kinder. Berlin ist weit weg und teuer. Im Theater läuft nur 2–3mal die Woche ein Kinofilm.

Und die Wochenenden? „Darüber kann man nicht viel sagen", meint Conny, eine 17-jährige Schülerin. Was hat sie denn am letzten
10   Wochenende gemacht? „Das war so langweilig, das weiß ich schon gar nicht mehr. Ich glaube, ich habe den ganzen Samstag im Bett gelegen und Fernsehen geguckt. Aber woanders ist es sicher auch nicht besser!"

Nur junge Arbeitslose freuen sich in Anklam auf das Wochenende. Denn dann trifft man jede Menge[1] Gleichaltriger: auf dem Marktplatz, auf der
15   Straße, an der Bushaltestelle, an der Tankstelle oder im *Onkel Ben*. So heißt die für Jugendliche einzige akzeptable Kneipe der Stadt. Hier wie überall gibt es fast nur ein Thema: Wer ist mit wem befreundet und seit wann? Neuigkeiten sind spätestens nach 2 Tagen bekannt.

Und was hat Conny an diesem Wochenende vor? Dieses Wochenende
20   muss Conny lernen, denn nächste Woche sind Prüfungen in der Schule. Lust aufs Lernen hat sie wenig, besonders Mathe ist für sie „der reine Horror". Aber weil sie ein schlechtes Gewissen[2] hat, verabredet sie sich mit einer Freundin zum Mathe-Üben bei sich zu Hause.

Sehr intensiv ist das Lernen nicht. Denn Conny macht auch an diesem
25   Wochenende alles, was sie normalerweise von Freitag bis Sonntag macht: Geburtstage feiern oder mit Freund Kristian in der Gegend rumfahren. Im Sommer trifft man sich meistens zum Grillen im Garten oder am See.

Kristian ist 19 Jahre alt. <u>Das ist wichtig, denn er hat einen Führerschein, ein Auto und sogar eine eigene Wohnung. Kristian benutzt sein Auto fast an</u>

30 <u>jedem Wochenende, um seine Mutter, die schwer krank ist, zu besuchen. Er fährt mit ihr spazieren, zum Einkaufen und Bekannte besuchen.</u>

Freitags geht er schon um 18 Uhr ins Bett, denn samstags arbeitet er von 0 Uhr bis 9 Uhr als Lehrling in einer Bäckerei. Wenn Kristian montags frei hat, „ist eigentlich nie etwas los[3]". Für andere dagegen bedeutet das Auto in

35 Anklam die „große Freiheit" – besonders am Wochenende. Mit einem Auto kann man in umliegende Städte und Dörfer fahren, die Disko wechseln und andere Leute treffen, im Sommer zum Schwimmen an die Ostsee fahren. Man kann auch im nahen Polen einkaufen gehen und dort sind Zigaretten besonders billig.

40 Auch Kathrin, 17, und Mandy, 16, arbeiten am Wochenende. Kathrin macht eine Lehre als Floristin und steht bis Samstagnachmittag im Geschäft. An diesem Wochenende ist sie auch am Sonntag da: weil Muttertag ist, brauchen viele einen Blumenstrauß. Mandy ist Schülerin und jobbt am Wochenende in einem Altenheim[4]. „Telefondienst machen und an der

45 Rezeption sitzen ist nicht anstrengend. In den letzten 5 Stunden ist niemand gekommen, und niemand hat angerufen."

Nach der Arbeit gehen Kathrin und Mandy in eine der 3 Spielotheken der Stadt. Sie hoffen, Bekannte zu treffen. Der Eintritt ist zwar für Jugendliche unter 18 nicht erlaubt, aber das nimmt man in Anklam nicht so genau.

50 Kathrin und Mandy spielen mit Vorliebe Billard oder Darts. Dafür und für andere Spiele brauchen sie viel Geld, denn kein Spiel ist kostenlos. Bowling spielen nur Erwachsene. Und mit ihren Eltern unternehmen Kathrin, Mandy und all die anderen am Wochenende „eigentlich nie etwas". Zu Zeiten der DDR war das anders: Da hatten die Eltern im Beruf weniger

55 Stress und am Wochenende noch Zeit auszugehen. Heute arbeiten viele auch am Wochenende: Weil sie müssen oder weil es sich lohnt.

[1] jede Menge: loads of
[2] ein schlechtes Gewissen: a bad conscience
[3] (es)ist eigentlich nie etwas los: there is actually never anything going on
[4] das Altenheim: old people's home

QUESTIONS

1. Give details of any two free time activities on offer to teenagers in Anklam. **2 points**

2. The weekends can be very boring (lines 8–12).

   What does Conny vaguely remember doing last weekend? **2 points**

3. Read paragraph 3 (lines 13–18).

   (a) Why do the young unemployed look forward to the weekend? **1 point**

   (b) What are we told about *Onkel Ben*? **1 point**

   (c) What is usually the main topic of conversation? **1 point**

4. Now read lines 19–27.

   (a) How does Conny intend spending the coming weekend? **1 point**

   (b) Mention two things she would normally do at the weekend. **2 points**

5. Read the information about Kristian (lines 32–39).

   (a) Why does he go to bed at six o' clock on a Friday? **2 points**

   (b) Mention in detail three specific benefits of having a car in Anklam. **3 points**

6. Now read the information about Kathrin and Mandy (lines 40–46).

   (a) Why does Kathrin have to work this Sunday? **2 points**

   (b) Why does Mandy not find reception work stressful? **1 point**

7. In the last section (lines 54–56) we are told how things have changed for parents since the reunification of Germany. Mention two changes. **2 points**

   (20 points)

   = 20 marks

8. Translate into English:

   „Das ist wichtig . . . und Bekannte besuchen." (lines 28–31) **10**

   (30)

11

Passage 3

Read this magazine article carefully, then answer **in English** the questions which follow it. You may use a German dictionary.

A 16-year-old girl, Ingrid, sets out to find the father she has never known.

Ich verlor meine Mutter – aber fand meinen Vater

An mich und meine Mutter habe ich sehr schöne Erinnerungen[1]. Wir unternahmen viel zusammen, aber am liebsten denke ich an die Zeit zurück, in der wir in unserer Wohnung zu den alten Schlagern von Abba sangen und tanzten.

5   Mami und Papi trennten sich ein halbes Jahr nach meiner Geburt, also verdanke ich meine glückliche Kindheit meiner Mutter. Wir hatten so viel Spaß, dass ich nie einen Vater oder Geschwister vermisste. Manchmal fuhren wir am Wochenende nach London, zum Einkaufen oder um ins Museum zu gehen, anschließend[2] besuchten wir dann immer Verwandte. In
10   den Ferien fuhren wir oft ans Meer.

Dann fuhr ich zu meiner Oma, weil Mami ins Krankenhaus musste. Es war eine Routineoperation, also machte ich mir keine großen Sorgen. Aber eine Woche später rief das Krankenhaus an: Meine Mutter musste auf die Intensivstation verlegt[3] werden. Ich war geschockt – sie war doch nur wegen
15   eines ganz kleinen Eingriffs[4] im Krankenhaus gewesen! Oma und ich verbrachten die ganze Zeit am Bett meiner Mutter. Wir hofften und beteten, dass Mami durchkommen würde. Doch eine Woche später ist sie gestorben. Sie war erst 38 Jahre alt. Ich hätte nie gedacht, dass Mami mich verlassen könnte, und jetzt war ich plötzlich allein.

20   Erinnern konnte ich mich an meinen Vater natürlich nicht, ich war ja damals noch ein Baby gewesen, aber ich kannte ihn von den Fotos, die mir Mami gezeigt hatte. Ein paar Monate später erfuhr ich durch Zufall[5], dass die Heilsarmee auch bei der Suche nach vermissten Menschen helfen würde. Eine einzige Frage ging mir durch den Kopf: Wie sieht mein Vater wohl
25   heute aus? Doch dann stand mein Entschluss fest: Zusammen mit meiner Oma wollte ich mich nun endlich auf die Suche nach meinem Vater machen ...

Wir redeten sehr lange darüber, und schließlich stimmte meine Oma zu,

dass es eine gute Idee sei. Sie ging in meinem Namen zur Heilsarmee.
30 Dort erklärte man ihr, dass es manchmal recht schwierig sei, die gesuchte
Person zu finden, vor allem, wenn der Kontakt schon so lange abgerissen
sei wie bei mir und meinem Vater. Eine Ewigkeit verging, und wir hatten
noch keine Antwort. Ich gab die Hoffnung auf. Doch nach etwa sechs
Monaten bekam Oma einen Anruf in der Arbeit: Es war jemand von der
35 Heilsarmee, und es waren gute Nachrichten! Oma erzählte mir, dass sie
Kevin, meinen Vater, gefunden hätten und wissen wollten, ob ich ihn treffen
wolle. Ich hatte mir bisher noch keine Gedanken gemacht, wie es sein
würde, wenn ich meinen Vater tatsächlich träfe. Was wäre, wenn er
eine neue Familie hatte und nichts von mir wissen wollte? Tief in meinem
40 Innersten wusste ich aber genau: Ich würde es für immer und ewig bereuen,
wenn ich ihn jetzt nicht sehen würde. Also sagte ich zu meiner Großmutter:
„Okay, Oma, vereinbar ein Treffen mit ihm."

Am Samstagnachmittag war es soweit. Ich musste arbeiten, und der Tag
schien sich endlos hinzuziehen. <u>Als ich nach Hause kam, wusste ich, dass</u>
45 <u>er da sein würde – es gab kein Zurück mehr. Langsam schloss ich die</u>
<u>Tür auf und ging hinein. Ich hörte Stimmen aus dem Wohnzimmer. Dann</u>
<u>stand ich vor ihm – meinem Vater, den ich 16 Jahre lang nicht gesehen</u>
<u>hatte.</u> Es war so merkwürdig. Alles was ich sagen konnte, war „Hallo". Es
war lange nicht so bewegend, wie man sich das vielleicht denkt: keine
50 Tränen, keine innige Umarmung oder so – wir waren ja fast wie Fremde.
Kein Wunder, dass wir uns nicht sofort um den Hals fielen. Wir unterhielten
uns mehr als zwei Stunden und füllten gegenseitig die Lücken unseres
Lebens. Er war richtig süß und wollte alles über mich wissen: Wies in der
Schule lief, welche Hobbies ich hatte. Dann erzählte er über sich. Er lebte
55 gar nicht so weit weg und hatte keine Familie. Als mein Vater am Abend
ging, machten wir für Samstag ein nächstes Treffen aus.

Seitdem treffen wir uns fast jedes Wochenende. Er kommt oft zu Oma, und
ich war schon zweimal bei ihm. Diesen Sommer hat er mich nach Zypern
eingeladen. Obwohl ich meine Mutter verloren habe, hatte ich Glück, weil
60 mir Oma und meine Freunde geholfen haben, die Kraft aufzubringen,
meinen Vater zu treffen. Papi wird Mami zwar nie ersetzen können, aber es
macht viel Spaß, sich gegenseitig kennen zu lernen.

[1] die Erinnerung: memory
[2] anschließend: afterwards
[3] verlegen: to transfer, to move
[4] der Eingriff: operation
[5] durch Zufall: by chance

QUESTIONS

1. In paragraph 1 we are told of Ingrid's fond memories of her mother. What does she remember?   **2 points**

2. Ingrid owes her happy childhood to her mother.
    (a) Why did she never know her father?   **1 point**
    (b) What sort of things did she and her mother do together?   **2 points**

3. In lines 11–19 we are told of the events which changed her life forever.
    (a) Why did Ingrid have to go to her grandmother's?   **2 points**
    (b) What gave her reason for concern one week later?   **1 point**
    (c) What fact suggests that her mother's death was particularly tragic? **1 point**

4. Read paragraph 4 (lines 20–27).
    (a) What did she find out about the Salvation Army?   **1 point**
    (b) What was the one question which kept going through her head?   **1 point**

5. Ingrid's grandmother was of help during this time (lines 28–42).
    (a) What was she told by the Salvation Army officers?   **2 points**
    (b) When Kevin was finally found and Ingrid considered meeting him, which two thoughts went through her mind about him?   **2 points**
    (c) What did she ask her grandmother to do?   **1 point**

6. Ingrid's reunion with her father was not as emotional as you might expect (lines 48–56).

    How did they react to each other before they exchanged information?   **2 points**

7. What evidence is there in the final paragraph that her relationship with her father will continue to develop?   **2 points**

                                                                              20 points

                                                                              = 20 marks

8. Translate into English:

    „Als ich nach Hause kam ... lang nicht gesehen hatte."
    (lines 44–48)   **10**

                                                                              (30)

14

Passage 4

Read this magazine article carefully, then answer **in English** the questions which follow it. You may use a German dictionary.

In this article a young woman, Hannelore, talks about the problems she faced in having her mother come to live with her.

Meine Mutter behandelte mich wie ein Kind

Nach dem Tod[1] meines Vaters vor fünf Jahren zog meine Mutter zu mir. Wenn ich ehrlich bin, muss ich zugeben[2], dass ich damals ein ungutes Gefühl hatte. Meine beiden Schwestern Mona und Christa verstanden sich viel besser mit Mutter als ich. Auch sind beide verheiratet, leben in großen
5 Einfamilienhäusern und hätten eigentlich mehr Platz gehabt, um sie aufzunehmen, als ich in meiner kleinen Zweizimmerwohnung.

Doch als ich damals protestierte, meinte meine Mutter nur, wir könnten uns ja eine größere Wohnung mieten. Meine Schwestern sagten nichts dagegen. Sie wussten ja wie gutmütig ich war.

10 So hatten wir beide uns also eine größere Wohnung gemietet. Gleich zu Beginn unseres Zusammenlebens gab es Probleme. Angefangen beim Essen, das ich ihrer Meinung nach immer falsch zubereitete, über die Wäsche, die nur sie allein richtig sortieren konnte, bis hin zum selbst gemischten Futter für meinen Kater – Mutter wusste und konnte alles
15 besser.

Ein paar Mal besuchte sie mich in der Mittagspause im Betrieb und plauderte sogar mit meinem Chef über mich. Das war mir sehr peinlich. Zu Hause machte ich ihr deshalb Vorwürfe[3], woraufhin sie natürlich schmollte.

Das Schlimmste aber war, dass Mutter sich auch einmischte, mit wem
20 ich befreundet war. Ich fühlte mich mit meinen achtundzwanzig Jahren wie ein Schulmädchen.

Wenn ich samstagabends mit einem Freund ausging, stand sie hinter der Wohnungstür, fing meinen Bekannten ab und fragte ihn nach seinen Absichten aus. Klar, dass die meisten Männer mich nicht wiedersehen
25 wollten.

Ein paar Wochen später kam meine Mutter nach einem Arztbesuch völlig aufgelöst[4] nach Hause. Der Arzt riet zu strenger Diät, am besten verbunden mit einer Kur[5]. So packte sie ihre Koffer und machte sich auf den Weg nach Bad Oberstdorf.

30 <u>Nach ihrer Abfahrt lebte ich wieder, wie ich wollte jaß, was mir schmeckte, schlief am Samstag lange, fütterte den Kater mit Dosen und ging am Wochenende so lange aus, wie ich wollte.</u>

Und dann lernte ich Manfred kennen. Wir trafen uns auf der Geburtstagsfeier eines Kollegen. Ich unterhielt mich an diesem Abend nur 35 mit ihm, und wir kamen uns schnell nah.

Als wir uns verabschiedeten, hatten wir für den nächsten Tag eine Verabredung. Ich war bald verliebt in ihn, und als wir ein Paar wurden, war ich rundum glücklich.

Aber die Wochen vergingen, und dann kam der Tag, an dem Mutter aus der 40 Kur zurückkehrte. Ich hatte Angst davor, ihr etwas von Manfred zu sagen. Im Gegenteil zu mir hatte Manfred keine Angst vor meiner Mutter. Er konnte immer gut mit Menschen umgehen. Das bewies[6] er gleich beim ersten Zusammentreffen mit Mutter.

Es war Samstag und ich hatte Manfred zum Kaffee eingeladen. Meine 45 Mutter, die gerade einkaufen gehen wollte, blieb zu Hause und wartete auf ihn. Sie beobachtete ihn misstrauisch, aber ihre spitzen Bemerkungen fand er nicht beleidigend sondern lustig.

„Ein unverschämter junger Mann", war alles, was sie sagte, nachdem er gegangen war.

50 In der folgenden Zeit kam Manfred sehr oft zu uns und meine Mutter hatte die Gelegenheit, ihn wirklich gut kennen zu lernen. Sie begann, Manfred zu mögen, und schließlich verstanden sich die beiden recht gut.

Eines Tages kam ich von der Arbeit zurück nach Hause und fand eine völlig verwandelte Mutter vor: Nach einem intensiven Gespräch mit Manfred 55 hatte sie sich ein paar Gedanken um ihr Leben gemacht und war plötzlich der Meinung, ihre Zeit zu verschwenden. So hatte sie angefangen, sich in unserer Kirchengemeinde zu engagieren. Diese Aufgabe interessierte sie so sehr, dass sie überhaupt nicht mehr auf die Idee kam, sich in mein Leben einzumischen.

60 Heute bin ich wirklich glücklich. Ich fühle mich wieder im eigenen Zuhause wohl und hoffe nur, dass es noch lange so bleibt ...

[1] der Tod: death
[2] zugeben: to confess
[3] jemandem Vorwürfe machen: to reproach someone
[4] aufgelöst: distraught
[5] eine Kur: treatment at a spa
[6] beweisen: to prove

QUESTIONS

1.   In lines 1–9 we are told why Hannelore's mother came to live with her.

    (a)   What event prompted her mother to move in?   **1 point**

    (b)   Why did Hannelore think that her mother would have been better moving in with her other daughters?   **3 points**

    (c)   What solution did her mother come up with?   **1 point**

2.   There were domestic problems right from the start. Mention two specific areas of friction.   **2 points**

3.   Read lines 19–25.

    (a)   Domestic arrangements apart, how else did her mother interfere with her life?   **1 point**

    (b)   What did her mother do on a Saturday evening?   **2 points**

    (c)   What effect did this have on most of the men?   **1 point**

4.   Read lines 33–43.

    (a)   Where exactly did Hannelore meet Manfred?   **1 point**

    (b)   How do you know that they were attracted?   **2 points**

    (c)   Why did Manfred not fear meeting her mother?   **1 point**

5.   Manfred finally meets her mother (lines 44–52).

    (a)   How did he respond to her pointed remarks?   **1 point**

    (b)   Despite her mother's initial reservations, how did she respond to Manfred once she got to know him?   **2 points**

6.   Manfred helped her mother see her life differently (lines 53–59).

    (a)   What conclusion did she draw?   **1 point**

    (b)   Why did she finally leave her daughter alone?   **1 point**

(20 points)

= 20 marks

7.   Translate into English:

    „Nach ihrer Abfahrt … wie ich wollte." (lines 30–32)   **10**

(30)

Passage 5

Read this magazine article carefully, then answer **in English** the questions which follow it. You may use a German dictionary.

In this article a mother discusses her relationship with her drug-addicted son.

Mein Sohn ist ein Fixer

Evelyn Buchmann wird den 30. Geburtstag von Daniel nie vergessen. An diesem heißen Julitag gab die Mutter den Kampf[1] um ihr drogensüchtiges Kind auf. Sie schickte ihm keine Geburtstagskarte. Kein Geschenk. Es gab nur Tränen, Trauer, Resignation und unendliches Leid.

5 „Als ich mich entschloss, Daniels Geburtstag zum ersten Mal zu ignorieren, wußte ich, dass seine Sucht[2] uns beide zerstört hat", sagt Evelyn Buchmann.

15 Jahre hatte die 47-jährige versucht, stärker zu sein als Haschisch, Heroin und Methadon. 5475 Tage glaubte sie fest daran, ihren Sohn aus dem
10 Teufelskreis[3] Drogen herausreißen zu können.

Jetzt sitzen wir einer traurigen Frau gegenüber. Sie sieht blass und müde aus. Ihre Augen sind ohne Glanz. Nervös flatternde Hände. Jedes Erlebnis mit dem süchtigen Kind hat seine Spuren[4] hinterlassen. Energie, Optimismus – alles zerstört durch Daniels unbegreifliche Sucht.

15 Früher war Evelyn Buchmann Manager einer kleinen schweizer Baufirma. Heute lebt sie zurückgezogen in ihrer Penthouse-Wohnung über den Dächern von Aarau. Sie traut sich nicht einmal allein auf die Straße oder zum Einkaufen zu gehen: „Ich habe Angst, Daniel zu treffen. Ich kann nicht mehr ansehen, wie heruntergekommen mein Junge existiert, anstatt normal
20 zu leben."

Aarau ist eine kleine, idyllische Stadt mit 12 000 Einwohnern zwischen Zürich und Bern. Hier wirkt[5] alles sehr sauber und sehr ordentlich. „Aber das ist alles nur Fassade", sagt Evelyn bitter. „Hier ist alles mit Rauschgift verseucht[6]. Die städtische Drogenberatung ist völlig überlastet."

25 Damals, vor 15 Jahren, als Daniel dem Rauschgift verfiel, gab es noch keine Drogenberatung. „Das Problem wurde unter den Teppich gekehrt."

Mit wenigen Worten schildert Evelyn Buchmann die Vergangenheit. „Ich hatte es nie leicht. Mit 17 wurde ich schwanger und trug das Kind gegen den Willen meiner Mutter aus." Kein Wort über den Vater: „Ich wollte Daniel
30 allein großziehen."

Da Evelyn arbeiten musste und nicht viel Geld hatte, musste Daniel die ersten Jahre hauptsächlich bei der Oma verbringen. Von ihr wurde er völlig verwöhnt. „Sie betrachtete ihn als ihr Eigentum. Mit ihr konnte er machen, was er wollte, und sie schimpfte ihn nie, wenn er sich schlecht benommen
35 hatte. Mit mir versuchte er, genau so schwierig zu sein." Dann lernte sie einen Mann kennen, den auch Daniel vom ersten Tag an mochte. Erst jetzt wurde die Situation stabiler.

„Dino, mein Mann, ist die Liebe meines Lebens. Er hat alles miterlebt und mir immer wieder Kraft gegeben. Ohne ihn hätte ich nie so lange kämpfen
40 können."

Der langsame Zerfall der Familie fing mit einem Brief von Daniels Schule an. Evelyn erzählt: „Mit fünfzehn Jahren wurde er zum dritten Mal beim Rauchen erwischt und musste die Schule verlassen. Als ich versuchte, mit Daniel darüber zu reden, wurde er aggressiv und sagte, dass er sowieso
45 nicht länger in der Schule bleiben wolle. Es war ihm egal. Was konnte ich machen?"

Nachdem er aus der Schule hinausgeworfen wurde, war er eine Zeitlang arbeitslos. Evelyn versuchte, ihren Sohn zu ermutigen, aber er wurde immer deprimierter. Endlich fand er eine Lehre als Maler in einer Stadt
50 fünfzig Kilometer von Aarau entfernt. Daniel musste jeden Tag sehr früh aufstehen, um mit dem Zug zu fahren und kam erst um acht Uhr abends wieder nach Hause. Obwohl die Stunden sehr anstrengend waren, mochte Daniel die Arbeit, aber nach einer Auseinandersetzung mit seinem Chef schmiss[7] er seine Lehre und begann auf der Straße zu leben. Er fing an, sich
55 mit zweifelhaften Freunden herumzutreiben.

Seit Monaten hat Evelyn nichts von ihrem Sohn gehört: „Ich weiß heute, dass ich nichts mehr für meinen Sohn tun kann. Solange Daniel süchtig ist, will ich auch nichts von ihm wissen. Seine Sucht tut mir so weh. Aber ich bleibe immer seine Mutter."

[1] der Kampf: fight
[2] die Sucht: addiction
[3] der Teufelskreis: vicious circle
[4] die Spur: trace
[5] wirken: to seem
[6] verseuchen: to contaminate
[7] schmeißen: to chuck

QUESTIONS

1. In lines 1–10 we are told about Evelyn Buchmann's sadness.

   (a) Why will she never forget her son's 30th birthday? **1 point**

   (b) What showed her determination until this point and makes her defeat all the more tragic? **2 points**

2. Read lines 11–14. What evidence is there that Evelyn Buchmann has not only been affected emotionally, but physically too? **3 points**

3. Now read lines 15–20.

   (a) What was Evelyn's job? **1 point**

   (b) Why is she now reluctant to leave her flat? **2 points**

4. Evelyn's home town of Aarau is described (lines 21–26).

   (a) In what way is its appearance misleading? **2 points**

   (b) How was Daniel's drug addiction dealt with 15 years ago? **2 points**

5. Evelyn's mother helped to bring up Daniel (lines 31–37).

   (a) Why was this necessary? **2 points**

   (b) How was he treated by his grandmother? **3 points**

6. Before Daniel ended up living on the street he found a job (lines 49–55).

   (a) What did he work as? **1 point**

   (b) Why did he leave this job? **1 point**

(20 points)

= 20 marks

7. Translate into English:

   „Mit fünfzehn Jahren wurde er ... konnte ich machen?" (lines 42–46). **(10)**

(30)

21

EDUCATION AND WORK

Passage 6

Read this magazine article carefully, then answer **in English** the questions which follow.

This article is about living and working on a cruise liner.

Das Dream-Team vom Traumschiff

Sibylle stellt das Unterhaltungsprogramm der nächsten 14 Tage vor. Sie
trägt eine blaue Uniform und arbeitet als Internationale Hostess an bord
des britischen Kreuzfahrtschiffs „Caronia". Sie betreut[1] 621 Urlauber aus
aller Welt, die in Fort Lauderdale an Bord gegangen sind, um durch den
5   Panamakanal bis nach Acapulco zu schippern. Die meisten Gäste sind
Rentner. Für ihr Wohlergehen[2] sorgt eine 385-köpfige Mannschaft, darunter
25 Deutsche, Österreicher und Schweizer. Die meisten machen ihren Job
für begrenzte Zeit, um der Langeweile zu entfliehen oder beruflich
weiterzukommen. Viele empfinden die „Caronia" als Zuhause. „Eine
10   Heimat für Heimatlose", nennt sie Sibylle.

Sibylle lebt mit Mann und vier erwachsenen Töchtern in einer Kleinstadt in der
Nähe von Hannover. Um neben ihrer Tätigkeit als Ernährungsberaterin[3]
etwas zu erleben, arbeitet sie alle drei Monate auf der „Caronia". Als
Internationale Hostess ist sie die offizielle Gastgeberin an Bord. Jeden Tag
15   ab 8.30 Uhr organisiert sie Quizshows, begleitet Gäste bei Landausflügen
oder steht für Auskünfte bereit. Wenn das Orchester gegen ein Uhr nachts
im Ballsaal den letzten Cha-Cha-Cha spielt, endet ihr Arbeitstag. Dann
steigt sie todmüde die Treppen zu ihrer kleinen Kabine hinunter. Die Crew
wohnt im Bauch des Schiffes.

20   Sibylles Freundin Alexandra hat einen Freund, den sie vor zwei Jahren auf
See kennen gelernt hat. Er arbeitet auf einem anderen Kreuzfahrtschiff, der
„Queen Elizabeth 2". Die mehrmonatige Trennung überbrückt[4] das Paar mit
E-Mails. „Nach jeder Dienstrunde haben wir drei Monate gemeinsam frei",
erzählt Alexandra. „Wenn wir zusammen sind, reisen wir oder wir
25   verbringen die Zeit in unserer gemeinsamen Wohnung in Köln."

„Wir haben den besten Job der Welt", schwärmt[5] Alexandras Freundin
Esther. Crew-Steward Esther ist für die Müllentsorgung und für die
Unterkünfte der Mannschaft zuständig. Sie ist 36, kommt aus Lübeck und

30 arbeitete bis 1994 als Biologie-Laborantin. „Wenn ich die Alltagsprobleme
meiner Freunde an Land sehe, frage ich mich, ob ich das haben muss",
meint sie. Rechnungen bezahlen, Wäsche waschen, Einkaufen, Kochen.
Das ist nichts für Esther.

Birgit, 24, kommt aus Wien und arbeitet als Barfrau. Seit zwei Jahren fährt
Birgit auf dem schwimmenden Hotel mit. Mit Trinkgeld verdient sie 2500
35 Dollar im Monat. „Was ein gutes Gehalt ist, weil man auf dem Schiff kaum
etwas ausgibt." Die Panama-Tour begleitet Birgit nun schon zum sechsten
Mal. Die „ständige Wiederholung" nervt sie inzwischen. Die Müdigkeit, die
sie spürt, wenn sie bei Seegang hinter der Bar die Balance hält. Die
Kabine, die sie mit wechselnden Kolleginnen teilt, geht ihr auf die Nerven.
40 Die Schwierigkeiten, eine Beziehung zu führen. Einige Male probierte Birgit
eine Beziehung an Bord, aber Schiffslieben gehen oft an Land schief.

Nach ein paar Monaten an Bord, hat Katrin versucht, wieder in der Schweiz
zu arbeiten, aber sie ist letztlich aufs Schiff zurückgekommen. Die schlechte
Bezahlung an Land und die miesen Aufstiegschancen als Köchin waren zu
45 deprimierend. Die 27-jährige sitzt jetzt in ihrer Kabine, in der man sich bei
hohen Wellen „wie in einer Waschmaschine fühlt". An der Wand hängt die
Weltkarte. Auf dem kleinen Bett liegt ein Teddy. Katrins Weg zur Arbeit
dauert zwei Minuten; zwei Stockwerke tiefer befindet sich die Küche. Die
ehemalige Metzgerin mit den blonden Haaren macht als Chef die Ansagen
50 in der Küche. 35 Männer kochen nach ihrem Kommando. Eine
ungewöhnliche Karriere für eine Frau. Dafür hat sie zwölfstündige
Arbeitstage. „Was ich vermisse, sind Rockkonzerte und meine Freunde",
erzählt sie.

Das Leben auf der „Caronia" läuft wie ein Uhrwerk. Vom ersten Frühstück
55 bis zum Mitternachtsbüffet tischt die Crew neun Mahlzeiten auf. Pro Jahr
werden zum Beispiel sieben Tonnen Schrimps, 22 546 Flaschen Wein und
drei Millionen Teebeutel verbraucht.

Das Schiff nähert sich Acapulco. Sibylle besichtigt am vorletzten Tag mit
den Passagieren die Brücke. Alexandra organisiert die Abreise der Gäste.
60 Birgit fährt die zweite Schicht an der Bar. Katrin steht zwischen dampfenden
Töpfen und brüllt Kommandos.

Am Abend steigt eine Party für die Crew. Einige halten drei Bierdosen
gleichzeitig in der Hand. Sie trinken alle bis sechs Uhr morgens zu viel.
„Wir haben alle Probleme und sind vor etwas davongelaufen", meint der 30-

65   jährige Crew-Steward Oliver. „Vor einer unglücklichen Liebe, vor einer
      kaputten Ehe oder einer beruflichen Pleite." Das Schiff fährt durch die
      Nacht. Nichts scheint in diesem Moment weiter weg als die Probleme in der
      Heimat.

[1] betreuen: to be in charge of
[2] das Wohlergehen: welfare
[3] Ernährungsberaterin: nutritionist
[4] überbrücken: to get through
[5] schwärmen: to enthuse

QUESTIONS

1. In the opening paragraph what are we told about most of the passengers on board the *Caronia*?   **1 point**

2. Why do most of the crew do this job for a limited time?   **2 points**

3. Read about Sibylle in paragraph 2 (lines 11–19).

   (a) As the official 'hostess' on board, mention two things her job involves.   **2 points**

   (b) What exactly are her working hours?   **2 points**

4. Read paragraph 3 (lines 20–25).

   How do Alexandra and her boyfriend spend their leave together?   **2 points**

5. Read the information about Esther (lines 26–32).

   (a) What are her duties on board?   **2 points**

   (b) Mention two chores she does not miss having to do back home.   **2 points**

6. Read paragraph 5 (lines 33–41).

   (a) Why does Birgit consider her salary a good one?   **1 point**

   (b) Mention two things which annoy her on board.   **2 points**

7. Read the information about Katrin (lines 42–53).

   (a) Why is her career as chef unusual for a woman?   **2 points**

   (b) Mention one drawback in this job.   **1 point**

8. In the final paragraph Oliver claims that each member of the crew is running away from problems.
   Mention one such problem.   **1 point**

                                                                        (20 points)

                                                                        = 20 marks

9. Translate into English:

   „Nach ein paar Monaten … waren zu deprimierend." (lines 42–45).   **10**

                                                                        (30)

Passage 7

Read this magazine article carefully, then answer in English the questions which follow.

Jean-Baptiste, a French student, arrives in Germany to spend one semester at a university.

Ein Semester fern der Heimat

Jean-Baptiste, 22, ist Franzose. Er studiert in Frankreich Maschinenbau[1]. Ein Semester verbringt er mit einem Stipendium der Europäischen Union an der Ruhr-Universität Bochum. Sie ist die Partneruniversität seiner Heimatuniversität Belfort, die das Semester im Ausland organisiert hat.

5 Dienstagabend, 21 Uhr 42 am Bahnhof Bochum: Jean-Baptiste steigt aus dem Intercityexpress. Er trägt eine schwere Reisetasche. Über seiner Schulter hängt eine Gitarre. Er sucht ein Telefon und ruft Hanna an. Vor seiner Abreise hat er ihre Telefonnummer bekommen. (Hanna ist eine deutsche Studentin, die schon einmal mit dem Erasmus-Programm der
10 Europäischen Union im Ausland war.) Hanna sagt: „Hallo. Ich hole dich ab und bin gleich da!"

Nach zehn Minuten kommt eine junge Frau direkt auf ihn zu. Gemeinsam gehen sie zum Parkplatz vor dem Bahnhof. Dort wartet Christian, 25, in einem alten Mercedes. Er ist Maschinenbau-Student wie Jean-Baptiste.
15 Alle drei fahren zum Studentenwohnheim, in dem Jean-Baptiste die nächsten 6 Monate wohnen wird. Es heißt *Haus der Nationen*. Die Universität hat hier ein Zimmer für ihn reserviert. Die Fahrt dauert länger, als Jean-Baptiste dachte: Die Ruhr-Universität ist eine Campus-Universität und liegt wie das Studentenwohnheim außerhalb der Stadt – ein Vorteil für
20 Jogger wie Jean-Baptiste.

Als sie ankommen, ist es draußen dunkel. Mit dem Aufzug geht es in den 4. Stock. An der Wohnungstür hängen drei Namensschilder. Auf einem steht Chris, auf dem anderen Thomas. Neben jedem Namen steckt ein kleines deutsches Fähnchen. Jean-Baptiste wird die französische Trikolore neben
25 sein Namensschild stecken. So sieht jeder, woher er kommt. Im *Haus der Nationen* wohnen ausländische Studierende mit Deutschen zusammen. Jean-Baptiste findet das „nicht nur wegen der Sprache" prima: „So lernt man sofort Deutsche kennen!" Alle haben ein eigenes Zimmer; jeweils[2] drei Studierende teilen sich eine Küche, eine Toilette und ein Bad. Das Zimmer
30 von Jean-Baptiste ist groß und sauber. Es gibt sogar einen kleinen Balkon. Das Bett ist gemacht. Trotzdem ist er ein bisschen enttäuscht, weil seine Mitbewohner nicht zu Hause sind: Sie verbringen die vorlesungsfreie Zeit bei ihren Eltern.

Hanna und Christian nehmen ihn mit in die Studentenkneipe. Sie ist um
35 diese Zeit gut besucht. Jean-Baptiste unterhält sich mit deutschen
Kommilitonen[3] über die Unterschiede des Studiums in Frankreich und in
Deutschland: „In Frankreich haben wir 35 Unterrichtsstunden pro Woche,
in Deutschland sind es nur 20.“ Er bekommt von seinen Gesprächspartnern
erste Tipps für das Leben in Bochum.

40 Am nächsten Morgen trifft er sich mit anderen Studierenden des Erasmus-
Programms. Die Gruppe nimmt an einem 3-wöchigen Orientierungskurs[4]
teil – mit Theaterbesuchen, Musikabenden, der Besichtigung von Städten
wie Köln und Essen und einem Sprachkurs. Alle müssen deshalb eine
Sprachprüfung machen. Jean-Baptiste kommt in die höchste
45 Sprachniveau-Gruppe. Nun warten Themen wie „Ausspracheübung“,
„Hörverständnis“, „Lesestrategien“ oder „Reden im Alltag“ auf ihn. Am
Ende wird er „Fortschritte vor allem beim Wortschatz“ gemacht haben.

Mittags geht es in die Mensa[5]. Hier essen die Studierenden für wenig Geld.
Jean-Baptiste lobt die Auswahl und die Qualität des Essens, „sogar an die
50 Vegetarier hat man gedacht!“ Als Vorspeise wählt er einen Salat;
Hauptgericht ist ein Stück Fleisch mit Kartoffeln und Gemüse; zum Nachtisch
gibt es Quark mit Früchten.

Am nächsten Tag steht ein Stadtbummel auf dem Programm: In kleinen
Gruppen erkunden die Teilnehmerinnen und Teilnehmer des
55 Orientierungskurses Bochum. Jean-Baptiste ist mit Elisa und Luisa aus
Spanien unterwegs. Sie befragen Leute auf der Straße. Dabei erfahren sie
zum Beispiel, dass das Kneipenviertel in Bochum *Bermuda-Dreieck* heißt.

Am Ende hat der Orientierungskurs Jean-Baptiste viel gebracht: „Ich finde
mich jetzt allein in Bochum und an der Uni zurecht, nun kann das
60 eigentliche Studium beginnen.“ Morgen hat er einen Termin bei seinem
persönlichen Betreuer[6]. Er ist Professor an der Fakultät für Maschinenbau.
Mit ihm wird Jean-Baptiste die Inhalte seines Studiums in Bochum festlegen
und die Kurse zusammenstellen. Das ist wichtig, damit das Semester in
Bochum an seiner Heimatuniversität anerkannt wird.

[1]	Maschinenbau:	engineering
[2]	jeweils:	at any one time
[3]	der Kommilitone:	fellow student
[4]	der Orientierungskurs:	organised student activities (similar to freshers' week)
[5]	die Mensa:	student refectory
[6]	der Betreuer:	adviser of studies

QUESTIONS

1. How did Jean-Baptiste end up studying engineering for a semester in Bochum? **2 points**

2. Read paragraph 3 (lines 12–20).
   (a) What do Christian and Jean-Baptiste have in common? **1 point**
   (b) Why does the journey to his destination take longer than Jean-Baptiste expected? **1 point**
   (c) Why is this an advantage for people like Jean-Baptiste? **1 point**

3. Read the information about his accommodation (lines 21–33).
   (a) What does Jean-Baptiste find on his door? **2 points**
   (b) What two advantages are there for foreign students like Jean-Baptiste in living here? **2 points**
   (c) What is his one disappointment? **1 point**

4. Hanna and Christian take Jean-Baptiste to the students' pub (lines 34–39).

   What does he talk about with the German students? **1 point**

5. Read how Jean-Baptiste will spend his first three weeks (lines 40–47).
   (a) Apart from the language course, mention any two planned activities. **2 points**
   (b) Mention two areas of study in his language course. **2 points**
   (c) In which area did he make most progress? **1 point**

6. Read the information about the student refectory (lines 48–52).

   Mention two things which impress Jean-Baptiste. **2 points**

7. Read the last two paragraphs (lines 53–64).
   (a) What do Jean-Baptiste and the two Spanish girls find out from the locals? **1 point**
   (b) Why is it important for Jean-Baptiste to sort out his course with his adviser of studies? **1 point**

   (20 points)

   = 20 marks

8. Translate into English:

   „Jean-Baptiste steigt aus ... Telefonnummer bekommen." (lines 5–8) **10**

   (30)

28

Passage 8

Read this magazine article carefully, then answer **in English** the questions which follow it. You may use a German dictionary.

This article is about holiday jobs for students in Germany and abroad.

Ferienjobs für Studenten

Jobben hat viele Vorteile. Manche Leute nutzen die Erfahrung als Sprungbrett für den späteren Beruf. Besonders in den Sommermonaten gibt es viele Möglichkeiten – nicht nur in Deutschland, sondern auch im Ausland. Sie können in attraktiven Feriengebieten arbeiten, ihre
5 Sprachkenntnisse auffrischen oder erweitern und interessante Einblicke in Alltag und Kultur eines anderen Landes bekommen.

Generell wichtig: Kümmern Sie sich rechtzeitig[1] um einen Job. Denn: Die besten Angebote sind schnell vergeben.
Hier berichten vier junge Leute über ihre Erfahrungen mit Sommerjobs im
10 In- und Ausland[2].

Sabine, 28.
Die Idee, als Animateurin[3] zu arbeiten, kam spontan: Bei einem Urlaub auf Fuerteventura fragte ich einfach beim örtlichen Club an. Ich bekam einen Job für die Ferien, lernte Spanisch – und los ging es: Tagsüber Wanderungen organisieren, Sprachkurse geben, bei der Strandgymnastik
15 mitturnen ... Animation heißt Gästekontakt pur – rund um die Uhr. Viel Spaß haben mir die Shows gemacht – von *Cats* bis *Starlight Express* war alles geboten. Nachdem ich mein Studium in Deutschland beendet hatte, bin ich zurückgefahren und noch einige Jahre geblieben. Die Zeit auf der Insel war die beste, die ich jemals hatte, und ich hatte Glück: Durch meine
20 Erfahrungen fand ich einen Job bei einer Fluggesellschaft.

Claudia, 24.
Um mein Jurastudium zu finanzieren, jobbe ich immer wieder als Kellnerin. Dabei habe ich schon wahnsinnig nette Leute kennen gelernt. Wir sind eine große Clique hier in Bonn und halten sehr zusammen. Am liebsten arbeite ich in einem vegetarischen Restaurant. Meine Aufgaben: Tische decken,
25 die Planung der verschiedenen Gerichte sowie das Abkassieren. Da ich mich selbst vegetarisch ernähre, bekomme ich dort eine Menge Anregungen[4]. Das Angebot ist unglaublich vielfältig, jeden Tag gibt es

etwas anderes. Und ganz toll dabei: Was übrig bleibt, können wir mit nach
Hause nehmen – in unserer WG[5] findet dann jedesmal eine Riesenfete statt.

Thomas, 25.

30 Ich habe diesen Job schon während meines Studiums gemacht. Über
einen Radiosender erfuhr ich damals, dass Stadtführer im Raum Würzburg
gesucht würden. Ich meldete mich, machte eine kleine Ausbildung
(Geschichte der Stadt, Kunstgeschichte) und führe seitdem die
unterschiedlichsten Gruppen durch meine Heimatstadt – von japanischen
35 Touristen bis zu den Teilnehmern an einem Ärztekongress. Diese Arbeit
bereitet mich auf meinen Beruf als Diplomkaufmann[6] vor: Der Umgang mit
Menschen macht viel Spaß. Oft werde ich noch in schicke Restaurants
eingeladen, dabei habe ich sehr gut gegessen.

Sonja, 25.

Ich dolmetsche jetzt seit fünf Jahren – immer in den Ferien. Da ich
40 zweisprachig (deutsch/italienisch) aufgewachsen und sehr an Sprachen
interessiert bin, dachte ich, ich könnte damit gut Geld verdienen. Also ließ
ich mich beim Arbeitsamt registrieren – und bekam bald meinen ersten Job.
Jetzt arbeite ich mit einer italienischen Agentur zusammen – sie vermittelt mir
die Firmenkunden. Mittlerweile habe ich auf allen Düsseldorfer Messen[7]
45 gearbeitet. Meine Aufgabe: Simultan-Dolmetschen. Ich bin bei
Geschäftsverhandlungen dabei, übersetze aus dem Stegreif[8]. Das erfordert
höchste Konzentration – für mich ein tolles Gedächtnistraining.
Stellenangebote hat man mir schon viele gemacht – erst kürzlich wollte mich
eine italienische Chemiefirma einstellen. Aber ich beende erst mal mein
50 Studium. Wer weiß, was danach kommt – Kontakte habe ich genug.

Ein paar Tipps

1. Es macht einfach mehr Spaß zu zweit zu jobben. Überlegen Sie sich, ob
Sie für Ihren Sommerjob nicht auch einen Freund oder eine Freundin
begeistern können!
2. Man muss rechtzeitig[1] daran denken. Alle notwendigen Papiere
55 (gültigen Pass usw.) schon einige Wochen vor Job-Beginn besorgen.
3. Wer ins Ausland geht, benötigt eventuell Impfungen oder bestimmte
Medikamente, die einige Zeit vor Reisebeginn arrangiert werden
müssen. Man muss beim Arzt nachfragen.
4. Erholen ist sehr wichtig. Jobben Sie nicht die ganzen Ferien über,
60 sondern planen Sie auch ein wenig Urlaub ein, bevor Ihr normaler
Alltag wieder losgeht.

1	rechtzeitig:	in good time
2	im In- und Ausland:	at home and abroad
3	Animateurin:	holiday group leader
4	eine Anregung:	an idea
5	eine WG (Wohngemeinschaft):	a shared flat or house
6	Diplomkaufmann:	qualified salesman
7	eine Messe:	a trade fair
8	aus dem Stegreif	off the cuff

QUESTIONS

1.   Mention three advantages of working in the holidays.   **3 points**

2.   Why is it important to organise your job in good time?   **1 point**

3.   Now read the information about Sabine (lines 11–20).

    (a)   How did she get her job on Fuerteventura?   **1 point**

    (b)   Mention two things her work involved during the day.   **2 points**

4.   Now read the information about Claudia (lines 21–29).

    (a)   Where exactly does she work?   **1 point**

    (b)   Mention two things her work involves.   **2 points**

    (c)   What are we told about the food on offer?   **1 point**

    (d)   What is the big advantage in working here?   **1 point**

5.   Now read about Thomas's job (lines 30–38).

    (a)   What does he work as?   **1 point**

    (b)   What did he learn on his training?   **2 points**

    (c)   How is he often thanked for his work?   **1 point**

6.   Now read the information about Sonja (lines 39–50).

    (a)   Why is she particularly suited to this kind of work?   **1 point**

    (b)   Why does she not accept the full-time job offers?   **1 point**

7.   Now read the tips given (lines 51–61).

    (a)   Why are those working abroad advised to see a doctor?   **1 point**

    (b)   What must you do before you get back to your everyday routine?   **1 point**

(20 points)

= 20 marks

8.   Translate into English:

„Nachdem ich mein Studium ... bei einer Fluggesellschaft." (lines 17–20)   **10**

(30)

Passage 9

Read this magazine article carefully, then answer **in English** the questions which follow it. You may use a German dictionary.

This article is about job prospects for young Germans who leave school with few qualifications.

Lust auf Zukunft

Annette, 17, hat beim Unterricht oft gefehlt. Sie ging lieber ins Kino oder in die Stadt. Während der Schulzeit war sie meistens bei ihrer besten Freundin Daniela zu Hause. Sie sagt: „In meiner Klasse haben fast alle geschwänzt[1]." Die Folge: Annettes Noten wurden immer schlechter. Sie
5   musste die Schule mit 16 Jahren verlassen. Mit ihren Eltern verstand sie sich nicht gut. Annettes Leben änderte sich, als sie ihren Freund Sven, 21, kennen lernte. Er ist Installateur und hat einen positiven Einfluss auf sie: „Wenn er sagte, geh zum Unterricht, habe ich das akzeptiert." Schließlich zog sie mit 17 Jahren zu ihrem Freund in eine gemeinsame Wohnung, die
10   im Haus von Svens Eltern liegt. Ihre Eltern hatten nichts dagegen. Heute geht Annette in Bonn auf eine Berufsschule. Sie begann mit einer Orientierungszeit[2]: Annette sah sich jeweils drei Wochen in einem anderen Berufsbereich um. Sie testete die Bereiche „Maler und Lackierer", „Hauswirtschaft" und „Körperpflege".

15   Die Wahl danach war leicht: Der Bereich „Körperpflege" gefiel Annette am besten. Frisieren, Maniküre und Kosmetik gehören dazu. Annette vertiefte ihre Kenntnisse und bekam die Chance gleichzeitig den Hauptschulabschluss nachzuholen. Das dürfen nur wenige: Die Teilnahme am Unterricht muss Erfolg versprechen. Über ein Praktikum fand
20   Annette einen Ausbildungsplatz[3] in einem Friseursalon. Sie verstand sich sofort mit dem Chef und mit den Kollegen. Die Arbeit war „genau das Richtige" für sie. Während ihrer Zeit in Bonn hat Annette nie gefehlt. Die strengen Regeln waren hierfür[4] nicht der Grund. Es hat ihr vielmehr Spaß gemacht. Und schließlich wollte sie sich ihre Zukunft nicht verderben.

25   Manuel, 21, ging nach dem Realschulabschluss auf ein Gymnasium. Dort waren seine Noten nicht sehr gut. Besonders in Deutsch und in Mathematik fiel ihm das Lernen schwer. Schließlich verließ er die Schule ein Jahr vor dem Abitur.

Sein Berufswunsch damals: Hotelkaufmann. Doch das Praktikum in einem
30   Hotel gefiel Manuel nicht. Er brach es nach drei Wochen ab. Mittlerweile

war es für die Bewerbung um einen anderen Ausbildungsplatz zu spät. Manuel jobbte ein Jahr lang circa 50 Stunden im Monat in einem Supermarkt. Nebenbei hatte er viel Freizeit. „Zu viel", wie er heute sagt. Seine Freunde arbeiteten den ganzen Tag und hatten deshalb nicht viel Zeit

35 für ihn. Manuel heute: „Es war total langweilig!" Manuels Eltern mischten sich nicht ein. Sie sagten: „Dein Beruf geht nur dich etwas an." Schließlich informierte sich Manuel beim Arbeitsamt über seine Berufsmöglichkeiten und -aussichten. Ergebnis der Gespräche und Tests: Manuel sollte sich für eine Ausbildung als Außenhandelskaufmann[5] bewerben. In diesem Beruf

40 sind seine Fremdsprachenkenntnisse nützlich.

Die Vorstellungsgespräche bei verschiedenen Firmen liefen laut Manuel gut. Dennoch bekam er keine Stelle: „Vielleicht waren meine Noten zu schlecht." Plötzlich war Manuel 20 und ein Beruf nicht in Sicht. Manuel bewarb sich[6] beim Institut für schulische und berufliche Bildung. Das ist

45 eine private Organisation, die Jugendliche auf die Ausbildung in kaufmännischen Berufen vorbereitet. Nach dem ersten Betriebspraktikum wusste Manuel: Ein 8-Stunden-Tag im Büro ist nicht für ihn. Jetzt interessierte er sich für eine Ausbildung zum Einzelhandelskaufmann[7]. Dabei sitzt man nicht immer nur im Büro und auch die Arbeitszeiten sind

50 flexibler. Manuel fand seinen Ausbildungsplatz selbst: Im Supermarkt, in dem er seit zwei Jahren jobbt. Kein Traumberuf, aber den hat Manuel sowieso nicht.

Jochen, 16, wurde wegen schlechter Noten zweimal nicht in die nächste Klasse versetzt. Schließlich war Jochen viel älter als alle anderen Schüler

55 seiner Klasse. Einen Hauptschulabschluss darf Jochen nicht machen. Sein Testergebnis war zu schlecht. Aber das ist ihm egal: Über einen Freund bekam er ein Praktikum und sogar einen Ausbildungsplatz als Metallbauer. Klar, dass er im Metallbereich bleibt. Ihm gefällt daran vor allem die Arbeit draußen: „Zum Beispiel Bushaltestellen aufbauen oder Fensterrahmen auf

60 Baustellen einsetzen." Jochen meint: „Warum brauche ich einen Schulabschluss, wenn ich eine Lehrstelle und danach vielleicht einen Arbeitsplatz habe?"

[1]	schwänzen:	to play truant
[2]	eine Orientierungszeit:	taster courses
[3]	der Ausbildungsplatz:	training vacancy
[4]	hierfür:	for this
[5]	Außenhandelskaufmann:	exporter
[6]	sich bewerben:	to apply
[7]	Einzelhandelskaufmann:	retailer

QUESTIONS

1. Read the information about Annette in paragraph 1 (lines 1–14).

    (a)   Where was she when she should have been at school?   **2 points**

    (b)   What was the consequence of this?   **2 points**

    (c)   In what way did Sven have a positive influence on her education?   **1 point**

    (d)   Mention two courses of study offered at Annette's college.   **2 points**

2. Read lines 15–24.

    (a)   Why was Annette lucky to be given the chance to work for the *Hauptschule* exams?   **1 point**

    (b)   What does this tell us about her work at the college?   **1 point**

    (c)   Why did Annette never skip classes here?   **2 points**

3. Read paragraphs 3 and 4 (lines 25–40).

    (a)   Why did Manuel leave school?   **2 points**

    (b)   Why did he not enjoy his free time when he worked in the supermarket?   **2 points**

    (c)   What was his parents' attitude towards his career?   **1 point**

4. Now read lines 43–52.

    (a)   What did Manuel realise after his first placement in a business?   **1 point**

    (b)   Mention one advantage of working as a retailer.   **1 point**

5. Now read the information about Jochen (lines 53–62).

    (a)   Why does he like working with metal?   **1 point**

    (b)   Mention one typical task in his line of work.   **1 point**

                                                                                               (20 points)

                                                                                               = 20 marks

6. Translate into English:

    „In diesem Beruf ... nicht in Sicht." (lines 39–43)   **10**

                                                                                               (30)

Passage 10

Read this magazine article carefully, then answer **in English** the questions which follow.

Clara considers the consequences of having to repeat a school year.

Warten auf den blauen Brief

Wenn ich in der nächsten Woche noch mal eine Sechs in Latein bekomme, weiß ich, was kurz vor den Zeugnissen mit der Post kommen wird: ein blauer Brief.

Eine Woche vor dem Zeugnis wird es eine große Lehrerkonferenz geben.
5   Und dann werden die blauen Briefe verschickt. Davor habe ich schreckliche Angst. Angst, schwarz auf weiß zu lesen, dass ich sitzen bleibe. Als ich dieses Schuljahr zum ersten Mal eine Sechs geschrieben habe, musste ich schon den ganzen Nachmittag heulen. Ich konnte das nicht glauben: eine richtige Sechs – „ungenügend". Vorher, in der fünften Klasse, war ich in
10   Latein zwar auch nicht gut – aber es gelang mir, mich so durchzumogeln[1]. Ich lernte ein bisschen Vokabeln, vor der Klassenarbeit wiederholte ich etwas mehr. Grammatik habe ich kaum gepaukt, sie war mir viel zu kompliziert, sie habe ich gehasst. Die Quittung dafür kam dann im letzten Zwischenzeugnis[2]. Latein: Sechs, weil ich gar nicht mehr Schritt halten[3]
15   konnte mit dem Unterrichtsstoff. Da wurde mir das erste Mal klar, dass ich sitzen bleiben könnte. Das war ein richtiger Schock. Sitzen bleiben doch nur die Doofen, dachte ich. Es wäre ungerecht. Ich bin doch gar nicht so schlecht in der Schule! In Mathe bekomme ich sogar gute Noten.

Eine Klasse zu wiederholen, das stelle ich mir ziemlich schrecklich vor.
20   Alles wird noch mal wiederholt: Pflanzen und Tiere in Biologie, in Deutsch einen Aufsatz über das gleiche Thema wie letztes Jahr. Meine Freundinnen kriegen viele neue Fächer: Sie lernen dann zum Beispiel Englisch und werden die Gelegenheit haben, einen Austausch nach England zu machen, und ich habe mich so darauf gefreut! Wie kindisch die Schüler sind, neben
25   denen ich dann nächstes Jahr im Unterricht sitze. Ich bin nämlich sowieso schon ein Jahr älter, weil ich erst nach der fünften Klasse Hauptschule aufs Gymnasium gekommen bin. Die Schüler in dieser neuen Klasse denken bestimmt, dass ich hoffnungslos bin, und wollen vielleicht nichts mit mir zu tun.

30 Ob meine Freundinnen eine Sitzenbleiberin auch mögen? Davor fürchte
ich mich am meisten: Dass sie den Kontakt abbrechen, wenn ich in eine
andere Klasse komme. Ich werde sie jeden Tag in der Schule nicht sehen.
Wir haben uns doch erst dieses Jahr so richtig angefreundet. Jetzt sind wir
noch eine feste Clique. Aber wenn wir nicht mehr zusammen Schule
35 aushaben und ganz andere Stundenpläne – ich glaube das wird schwierig.

Meine Eltern wissen, dass ich vielleicht sitzen bleiben muss. Sie sind wirklich
verständnisvoll und wir streiten uns nicht darüber zu Hause. Ich glaube, das
habe ich meiner Klassenlehrerin zu verdanken. Sie hat sich mit meiner
Mutter unterhalten und hat sie auf mein Zeugnis vorbereitet. Vielleicht ist
40 meine Mutter auch froh, dass ich nicht mehr so viel mit meiner Clique
zusammen sein werde, wenn ich die Klasse wiederhole. Nach der
zweiten Lateinschulaufgabe habe ich Hausarrest bekommen und durfte
abends nicht mehr mit meinen Freundinnen weggehen. Absoluter Blödsinn,
abends macht man sowieso keine Hausaufgaben mehr! Dann haben meine
45 Eltern meinem Bruder befohlen, mir zu helfen. Der Witz ist nämlich: Mein
Bruder ist ein Latein-Genie und überhaupt gut in der Schule. Aber wir
haben uns gestritten und schließlich haben mir meine Eltern
Nachhilfestunden[4] bezahlt. Einmal in der Woche ist eine Lehrerin zu mir nach
Hause gekommen. Aber diese Stunden nützten auch nicht viel, weil mir
50 eben die Grundlagen[5] aus der fünften Klasse fehlen.

Mein Lateinlehrer ist allerdings ein furchtbarer Typ. Er mag mich nicht.
Einmal haben wir in der Klasse die neuen Vokabeln durchgesprochen, und
da war das lateinische Wort „clarus" dabei. Dieses Wort bedeutet „hell"
oder „intelligent". Da hat der Lateinlehrer zu mir herübergeschaut, weil ich
55 doch Clara heiße, und hat zu mir gesagt: „Vielleicht in diesem Fall[6] nicht."
Ich bin knallrot geworden.

Nun kann ich nur warten. Ich würde lieber nie erfahren, ob Sitzenbleiber-
Briefe wirklich blau sind ...

[1] durchmogeln: to bluff one's way through
[2] das Zwischenzeugnis: interim report
[3] Schritt halten: to keep up
[4] eine Nachhilfestunde(n): private tuition
[5] Grundlagen: basics
[6] in diesem Fall: in this instance

QUESTIONS

1. Read lines 1–18.

   (a) How did Clara respond when she got a 'six' for the first time? **1 point**

   (b) How did Clara manage to bluff her way through in the 'fifth year'? **2 points**

   (c) Why did she not spend much time swotting up her grammar? **2 points**

   (d) Why does she think it would be unfair for her to repeat the whole year? **2 points**

2. Clara considers the consequences of having to repeat a whole year (lines 19–29).

   (a) Mention two things which she will have to do again. **2 points**

   (b) Why will she be particularly disappointed not to study English? **2 points**

   (c) What reservations does she have about being in classes with younger pupils? **2 points**

3. Read lines 30–35.

   What is Clara most afraid of? **2 points**

4. Clara mentions her family (lines 39–50).

   (a) Why is her mother perhaps glad that she might have to repeat the year? **1 point**

   (b) How was she punished after the second piece of Latin homework? **1 point**

   (c) What action did her parents take to improve her grades? **1 point**

5. Clara mentions her Latin teacher (lines 51–56).

   (a) What exactly does she say about him? **1 point**

   (b) How did she respond when he humiliated her? **1 point**

   (20 points)

   = 20 marks

6. Translate into English:

   „Meine Eltern wissen … mein Zeugnis vorbereitet." (lines 36–39) **10**

   (30)

THE WIDER WORLD

Passage 11

Read this magazine article carefully, then answer **in English** the questions which follow.

Going on holiday with family friends may seem like a practical solution, but sharing a holiday house brings problems of its own.

Eine schrecklich nette Familie

Eine beliebte Interviewer-Frage lautet: Was würden Sie am liebsten auf eine einsame Insel mitnehmen? Die Antwort lautet manchmal: Meine Freunde. Millionen von uns fahren jedes Jahr mit unseren Freunden in Urlaub. Wir mieten ein Häuschen auf Korfu oder ein Apartment auf
5 Mallorca. Wir fahren zwei Wochen auf ein Segelboot im Mittelmeer.

Die Urlaubs-Wohngemeinschaft[1] ist beliebt wie nie. Es gibt viele Gründe dafür: Arbeitsteilung: „Wir kochen dann immer abwechselnd", Finanzen: „Es ist viel billiger und gemütlicher als im Hotel", Fremdsprachen-Mängel[2]: „Nein, wir können leider kein Französisch – aber Rolf und Evelyne sprechen
10 es perfekt" oder Pädagogik: „Für ein Einzelkind ist es gut, wenn es in den Ferien so was wie Großfamilie erlebt".

Sechs Erwachsene und fünf Kinder fahren zu einem wunderbaren, vielräumigen Ferienhaus, das zwischen Meer und Gebirge in Südfrankreich liegt. Evelyne möchte im Urlaub am liebsten in der Sonne liegen, Tennis
15 spielen und Flohmärkte in entlegenen Dörfern besuchen. Ihr Mann Rolf bleibt normalerweise gern im Bett mit Stapeln von amerikanischen Computerbüchern. Aber da nun sein Freund Linus dabei ist mit seiner Frau Wibke, wird er mit seinem Freund im Schatten sitzen und Pfeife rauchen, Schach spielen oder ein Buch schreiben ... Die Kinder wird man gar nicht
20 merken; schließlich ist die Oma dabei (sie passt gut auf die Kinder auf) und die kinderliebe Claudia ist auch dabei.

Gleich bei der Ankunft beginnt die Reiberei[3]. Rolf und Evelyne sprechen nicht halb so gut Französisch wie gedacht – man muß mit Händen und Füßen den Weg zum Ferienhaus erfragen. Claudia gibt es nicht offen zu,
25 aber man sieht es ihrem Gesicht an, dass sie viel lieber das große Zimmer mit Aussicht gehabt hätte als das kleine nach hinten. Außerdem muss sie gleich sagen, dass sie seit zwei Monaten Vegetarierin ist und kein Fleisch im Kühlschrank sehen möchte.

Beim Frühstück am dritten Tag scheint die Sonne. Ein deutsches Auto hält
30   vor der Tür und Sekunden später stehen Karin und Christian mit ihrem
Schäferhund[4] und Schlafsäcken auf der Matte und wollen erst mal duschen.
Aber der Boiler ist grad kalt. Warmes Wasser gibt es bei so vielen Leuten
immer nur nach Stundenplan. Oma blickt auf den Hund: „Kinder, ihr wisst
doch, dass ich eine Tierhaarallergie habe. Der Hund muss aus dem Haus!"
35   Er wird in den Campingbus gesperrt und fängt an zu jaulen. Claudia strahlt
unschuldig: „Ich dachte, es wäre eine schöne Überraschung, wenn meine
Freunde hier für ein paar Tage vorbeischauen." Evelyne zerrt[5] Rolf ins
Schlafzimmer und zischt[6]: „Claudia weiß ganz genau, dass wir Karin und
Christian nicht ausstehen können!"

40   Beim Abwaschen gibt es Probleme. Linus ist schlechter Laune und will
nicht abwaschen. „Es steht doch im Prospekt etwas von Spülmaschine,
oder?" sagt er. Seine Frau Wibke erklärt den anderen: „Er ist nur
schlechter Laune, weil er abnehmen muss und der Arzt ihm das Bier
verboten hat." Evelyne will auch nicht abwaschen. Sie hat eine
45   Waschmittelallergie. „Können nicht mal die Kinder?" fragt Oma. „Ich würde
ja gern, aber mir geht es nicht gut wegen dem vielen Knoblauch, den ihr
immer ans Essen tut. Ich bin es ehrlich gesagt auch nicht gewöhnt, so spät
zu essen. Außerdem habe ich ganz schlecht geschlafen auf dieser
buckligen Matratze."

50   Am siebten Tag bittet die Großmutter zum nächsten Bahnhof gefahren zu
werden. Es ist ihr zu heiß, zu laut, zu fremdländisch, „und keiner kümmert
sich wirklich um mich." „Ich will auch heim", mault Claudias Einzelkind
Florian. „Ich kann Sebastian und Ernestine und Markus und Leila nicht
ertragen. Ich hasse Segelkurse in Französisch, ich hasse Museumsbesuche
55   . . . Ich will zu meinem Computer und meine Freunde von der Skateboard-
Schanze sehen!"

Am nächsten Tag steigen sie alle in die Kombiwagen ein und kehren nach
Hause zurück. Sie sprechen nicht viel, weil sie alle müde sind. Außerdem
planen die Eltern, was sie nächstes Jahr machen werden. Evelyne und Rolf
60   gehen vielleicht allein mit den Kindern zelten, Linus und Wibke wollen mit
ihren Kindern eine Fahrradtour durch Holland machen. Claudia hat vor,
alleine nach Griechenland zu fahren und hofft einen neuen Partner zu
finden. Ihr Sohn kann seinen Vater besuchen. Und die Oma? Sie möchte
unbedingt zu Hause bleiben und gemütlich auf dem Balkon Zeitschriften
65   lesen.

[1] die Urlaubs-Wohngemeinschaft: shared holiday accommodation
[2] Fremdsprachen-Mängel: lack of proficiency in foreign languages
[3] die Reiberei: friction
[4] der Schäferhund: alsatian
[5] zerren: to drag
[6] zischen: to hiss

QUESTIONS

1. Which question is a favourite with interviewers? **1 point**

2. Mention two kinds of holiday we might spend with our friends. **2 points**

3. In paragraph 2 some of the advantages of going on holiday with friends are listed.

    (a) What financial benefit is mentioned? **1 point**

    (b) What advantage is there for an only child? **1 point**

4. Read lines 17–21.

    Mention two things Rolf intends doing with his friend. **2 points**

5. There is friction from the start (lines 22–28).

    (a) How do we know that Rolf and Evelyne do not speak French very well? **1 point**

    (b) Give two reasons for Claudia's discontent. **2 points**

6. Claudia has invited some guests (lines 29–39).

    (a) Why does Gran not want a dog in the house? **1 point**

    (b) Why is Evelyne annoyed that Claudia has invited Karin and Christian? **1 point**

7. No one wants to wash up (lines 40–49).

    (a) According to his wife, what is the real reason for Linus's bad mood? **1 point**

    (b) Why does Evelyne not want to wash up? **1 point**

    (c) Why is Gran feeling unwell? **2 points**

8. Read lines 50–56.

    Why does Florian want to go home? **2 points**

9. In the final paragraph the holidaymakers are considering next year's trips.

    Mention two of their plans. **2 points**

    20 points

    = 20 marks

10. Translate into English:

    „Sechs Erwachsene . . . Computerbüchern." (lines 12–17) **10**

    (30)

Passage 12

Read this magazine article carefully, then answer **in English** the questions which follow it. You may use a German dictionary.

Glasgow – eine freundliche Stadt

A journalist writes about his experiences of life in Glasgow.

Ich bin Journalist und wohne seit 30 Jahren hier in der größten Stadt Schottlands. Was ich über Glasgow denke und fühle ist sehr vielschichtig[1]. Was ich über Glasgow nicht weiß, würde mehrere Bücher füllen.

5 Glasgow ist hübsch und hässlich. Die Architektur der viktorianischen Innenstadt ist fabelhaft. Die Wohnblocks am Rande der Stadt sind entsetzlich. Glasgow ist eine harte Stadt, aber ich kenne Glaswegians, die sofort reagieren, wenn man das sagt. Und die typische Reaktion? „Also, jetzt hör mir gut zu. Ich habe mein ganzes Leben hier verbracht und habe in dieser Zeit zwei Schlägereien höchstens miterlebt. Natürlich gibt es hier
10 Gewalt, aber die gibt es schließlich überall." Sie haben da nicht unrecht. Gewalt ist viel dramatischer, als wenn nichts passiert, und deshalb immer für eine Geschichte in der Zeitung gut.

Eins ist klar. Die Leute sind freundlich. Vor einem Wohnblock in der South Side: Ein Fotograf, ein junger Journalist und ich wollen ein paar Fotos
15 machen. Wir brauchen Panoramaansichten von der Stadtmitte für ein Stück im „Herald". Vom sechzehnten Stock könnten wir vielleicht tolle Bilder machen. Wir gehen hinein. Vor dem Aufzug warten zwei ältere Frauen, eine jüngere und zwei kleine Jungs. Die beiden spielen Kopfball mit einem Tennisball. Der Ball kommt den anderen immer wieder gefährlich nahe.
20 Eine der älteren Frauen geht auf den Jungen zu: „Jetzt hör mal auf. Spielt doch draußen sonst spreche ich mit eurer Mutter!"
„Kein Problem, Alte", versichert einer der Jungs.

Auf dem Weg im Aufzug nach oben steigen nach und nach alle aus, bis auf die junge Frau und uns drei. Wir sprechen sie an und erklären, warum wir
25 hier sind. Wir möchten aufs Dach hinaus. Sie sagt, dass es im obersten Stock eine Tür nach draußen gibt. Allerdings wird sie wohl nicht offen sein. Sie wird immer abgeschlossen.

An der Tür angekommen sehen wir, dass die junge Frau recht hatte:

verschlossen. Wir gehen zum Aufzug zurück. Vor einer geöffneten Tür steht
30 die Frau. Sie hat ihrer Mutter von uns erzählt und jetzt wollen sie wissen, ob
wir nicht einfach von ihrem Balkon aus fotografieren wollen. Klar, wollen
wir.

Von da an wird der Tag richtig nett. Wir machen ruhig unsere Aufnahmen
und vom Balkon haben wir eine tolle Aussicht über das Stadtzentrum, den
35 Fluss und die vielen Parkanlagen. Als wir wieder hereinkommen, gibt es Tee
und Kekse. Wir unterhalten uns über die schrecklichen Nachbarn „oben",
das Leben in Hochhauswohnungen und wie es der Familie geht; dann
sehen wir uns das Fotoalbum von der Kanadareise der Tochter an.
Sie hat da nämlich ihre Schwester besucht, und natürlich sind wir ehrlich
40 erfreut, dass es ihr in Kanada so gut geht.

Diese Leute sind beeindruckend. Sie sind so vertrauensvoll. Vom ersten
Moment an vermitteln sie uns das Gefühl, wir hätten ein Recht, hier in dieser
Wohnung zu sein. Als wir uns verabschieden, sagt die Mutter, wir sollten auf
jeden Fall zurückkommen, wenn wir das nächste Mal in der Gegend sind.
45 Die ganze Begebenheit[2] ist ein unerwartetes Geschenk von vollkommen
fremden Menschen, die Fotos von Glasgow sind längst vergessen, ich bin
einfach nur froh, dass ich hierher gekommen bin.

Einmal stand ich an einer Bushaltestelle an der Great Western Road. Ich
weiß schon gar nicht mehr, was ich damals für Probleme hatte, auf jeden
50 Fall war ich total deprimiert. Plötzlich wurde ich von einem kleinen Mann
angesprochen. „Na, mein Junge? Du siehst aber gar nicht glücklich aus.
Du glaubst, du hast Probleme? Dann hör mir mal zu."

Allem Anschein nach[3] hat er ein paar Tage zuvor einen alten Freund
getroffen. Gemeinsam haben sie in Kneipen und Clubs stundenlang
55 getrunken und deshalb war der kleine Mann neben mir nächtelang nicht
nach Hause gekommen, um seine Frau und drei Kinder zu sehen. Nun
wollte er von mir wissen, was er tun sollte: gleich nach Hause gehen oder
vielleicht noch so eine Nacht in der Stadt?

Das sind die Augenblicke, in denen ich Glasgow wieder erkenne; eine
60 Stadt, in der es vielleicht schwierig ist, sich einsam zu fühlen.

[1] vielschichtig: complex
[2] die Begebenheit: episode
[3] allem Anschein nach: apparently

QUESTIONS

1. The journalist mentions two areas of Glasgow.

    How do they contrast?   **2 points**

2. How does a Glaswegian respond when he is told that Glasgow has the reputation of being
    a 'tough' city?   **2 points**

3. The journalist gives his own reason for this reputation.

    What comment does he make?   **2 points**

4. In paragraph 3 (lines 13–22), the journalist recounts an experience he had.

    (a)   What brought the journalist and his colleagues to the South Side of the city?   **2 points**

    (b)   What are the two boys doing at the lift?   **1 point**

    (c)   How does one of the elderly women make the boys stop?   **1 point**

5. Unable to gain access to the roof, the journalist and his colleagues are given another
    opportunity (lines 28–47).

    (a)   What does the young woman invite them to do?   **1 point**

    (b)   Why is this successful?   **1 point**

    (c)   Mention two of the topics of conversation over tea and biscuits.   **2 points**

    (d)   What does the mother say when the men are leaving?   **1 point**

6. The journalist mentions a man he once met on Great Western Road (lines 48–58).

    (a)   How was the journalist feeling at the time?   **1 point**

    (b)   Why did the stranger not want to go home?   **2 points**

    (c)   Which two options was the stranger contemplating?   **1 point**

7. In the final paragraph, how does the journalist describe Glasgow?   **1 point**

                                                                       20 points

                                                                       = 20 marks

8. Translate into English:

    „Auf dem Weg … draußen gibt." (lines 23–26)   **10**

                                                                       (30)

Passage 13

Read carefully the following magazine article, then answer **in English** the questions about it.

Four young Germans give an account of their time abroad where they attended language schools.

Sprachkurs

Julia

Die Stadt Hastings war voller Sprachschüler aus Deutschland, Spanien, Italien, Dänemark und Schweden. Um am Strand Leute kennen zu lernen, waren meine Freundin und ich gezwungen, Englisch zu sprechen. Und das war genau das, was ich mir von der Reise versprochen hatte. Auch mit
5   unserer total lieben Gastfamilie haben wir viel Englisch geredet. Das Wiederholen der Grammatik im Sprachkurs war mir nicht so wichtig, denn schriftlich bekam ich immer gute Noten in der Schule. Unsere Betreuerin[1], eine Engländerin, war unheimlich nett. Hilfreich war ein Treffen vor der Reise, auf dem wir Infos über den Unterricht und gute Tips für die
10   Reiseplanung bekommen haben. Falls ich noch mal eine Sprachreise mache, würde ich darauf achten, dass ich auf keinen Fall mit anderen Deutschen zusammen untergebracht werde. Dann ist man noch mehr zum Englischsprechen gezwungen.

Daniel

Ich musste unbedingt meine Fünf in Englisch verbessern und entschied mich
15   für die Insel Malta, weil ich dachte, dass ich dort nicht so vielen deutschen Sprachschülern begegnen würde. Ich fand einen Veranstalter, der mir eine internationale Klasse empfahl[2]. Überall auf Malta liefen Deutsche herum – in den Sprachschulen, in den Pensionen oder in der Jugendherberge, in der ich gewohnt habe. Das andere Problem war, dass nur wenige Malteser
20   die Amtssprache Englisch beherrschten. <u>Unsere Lehrer waren einheimische Studenten, deren Aussprache noch schlechter war als unsere. Im Unterricht hat man überhaupt nichts gelernt: zu den anderthalb Stunden Grammatik pro Tag gab es keine schriftlichen Übungen, und im Konversationsunterricht haben wir überwiegend Deutsch geredet.</u> Außerdem
25   war es unmöglich, sich bei Temperaturen um 40 Grad zu konzentrieren. Funktioniert hat nur die Partybetreuung – so gut, dass wir die meisten Morgen total schläfrig im Klassenraum saßen. Ich wusste sehr schnell: Hier bleibe ich keine drei Wochen. Das bringt einfach nichts. Nach einer Woche bin ich nach Hause zurückgeflogen.

Dieter

30 Ich dachte, ich könnte durch so eine Reise nach Südengland meine
Sprachhemmungen loswerden. Irrtum! Unser Lehrer war zwar fachlich gut,
aber er hat sich keine Mühe gegeben, ruhigere Schüler – wie mich – zum
Mitmachen zu animieren. Es war tierisch langweilig: in Gruppen mit je 16
Schülern haben wir endlos Grammatik gepaukt, aber viel zu wenig Englisch
35 gesprochen. Der ganze Unterricht wurde von drei Leuten dominiert. In
meiner Privatunterkunft ging es so unpersönlich zu wie in einem Hotel: Ich
wurde mit sieben Deutschen in einer Familie untergebracht. Über die Frage
„Was hast du heute gemacht?" ging das Interesse der Gasteltern nicht
hinaus. Überhaupt schienen die meisten Einheimischen von den vielen
40 Sprachschülern genervt zu sein, die jeden Sommer dort zusammen kommen.
So blieben wir Deutschen zusammen. Nett und engagiert waren allerdings die
Betreuer: Sie haben sich um jeden persönlich gekümmert.

Saskia

Meine Englischnote ist durch die vierwöchige Sprachreise nach Folkestone
noch nicht besser geworden, aber ich habe jetzt mehr Spaß am Unterricht:
45 Ich bin viel sicherer im Sprechen geworden und beteilige mich
entsprechend mehr. Wir waren nur zehn in der Gruppe, und unsere
englische Lehrerin hat überwiegend Hörübungen, Spiele und kleine
Theaterstücke mit uns gemacht. Da konnte niemand dem Sprechen
ausweichen. Obwohl wir nur 16 Unterrichtsstunden pro Woche hatten, war
50 das kein Erholungsurlaub. Es wurde unheimlich viel geboten: Auflüge nach
London und Cambridge, Sportfeste, Grill- und Spielabende, Feten. Meine
Gastfamilie hat mich nett umsorgt[3], wenn ich zu Hause war – was allerdings
tagsüber selten vorkam.

Ein paar Tipps

1. Für Jugendliche unter 15 Jahren ist unbedingt eine durchgehende
55 Betreuung während der Sprachreise notwendig. Aber auch wenn du älter
bist, solltest du vor der Reise klären, ob es am Schulort eine Kontaktperson
gibt, die rund um die Uhr erreichbar ist. Sie kann dir helfen, falls du mit dem
Kurs unzufrieden bist oder andere Probleme auftauchen.
2. Nimm dir Zeit für das Lesen des Vertrages. Wie viele Unterrichtsstunden gibt es
60 täglich? Wie ist die Unterkunft? Was sind die Freizeitangebote?
3. Überleg dir genau, was du dir von einem Sprachurlaub erhoffst.

[1] Betreuer(in): person in charge
[2] empfehlen: to recommend
[3] umsorgen: to look after

QUESTIONS

1. Read the paragraph about Julia (lines 1–13).

   (a) Why did Julia and her friend feel forced to learn English? **1 point**

   (b) Why was the revision of grammar not so important for her? **1 point**

   (c) Why was a meeting before the trip helpful? **2 points**

   (d) What would she pay particular attention to next time? **1 point**

   (e) What reason does she give for this? **1 point**

2. Now read the section on Daniel (lines 14–29).

   (a) Give details of the first problem he encountered on the island. **2 points**

   (b) Why was the weather a problem too? **2 points**

3. Now read Dieter's account (lines 30–42).

   (a) Why did he go to England? **1 point**

   (b) Why were the lessons boring? **2 points**

   (c) What comment does he make about the host parents? **1 point**

4. Now read about Saskia's experience (lines 43–53).

   (a) What positive effect did Saskia's stay have on her English? **2 points**

   (b) In what way were her teacher's lessons effective? **1 point**

5. A few tips are given for prospective students (lines 54–61).

   (a) Why is it important to have someone you can contact at any time while you are at the school? **1 point**

   (b) What information will be in the contract? **2 points**

   20 points

   = 20 marks

6. Translate into English:

   „Unsere Lehrer waren … Deutsch geredet." (lines 20–24) **10**

   (30)

ANSWER SCHEMES

Passage 1

Der Tag, an dem Papa fortging

1. Maren's father has left, but Maren thinks she may just have dreamt this (lines 4–9).

    What proof is there that her father has gone for good? **2 points**
    - there is a slip of paper on the bedside table
    - on which he has left his address

2. In paragraph 3 Maren thinks back over the day's events and her father's departure (lines 10–22).

    (a) Why was the big picture of the ship important to Maren? **1 point**
    - they were going to go round the world on a boat like it

    (b) How do we know that her father was upset? **1 point**
    - his face was wet (with tears)

    (c) When had Maren last seen her father in such a state? **1 point**
    - when her grandfather had died

    (d) What outings did he promise to go on with his daughter? **3 points**
    - they would visit her grandmother
    - they would go to Legoland
    - they would go to Disneyland Paris in the holidays

3. It was at family breakfasts that Maren first realised that things were not working out between her parents (lines 26–36).

    (a) What evidence was there that her parents had not slept well? **2 points**
    - her mother's eyes were puffy (she had been crying)
    - her father put twice as much sugar in his tea

    (b) Why had Maren not slept well again? **1 point**
    - her parents had been arguing (yelling at each other)

    (c) Maren's parents were not honest. How did they respond to her questions? **3 points**
    - they told her they were just fooling around
    - they told her she would not understand (not old enough yet to understand)
    - they evaded her questions and changed the subject

    OR
    - they asked instead about her homework or if she had tidied up

ANSWER SCHEMES

4. Maren thinks back to the time her parents told her they were splitting up (lines 37–46). How did her father try to reassure her? **2 points**

*   he told her their split had nothing to do with her
    (she was not to blame)
    *   she would visit him quite often at the weekend
    *   she was told she was a big, sensible girl
        (any 2)

5. We are given an insight into Maren's reaction to their separation (lines 47–54).

    (a) What conclusions does she draw? **2 points**
    *   her parents did not love each other enough any more
    *   perhaps her father was not leaving because of her mother
    *   perhaps he was leaving because she, Maren, was not lovable enough
        (any 2)

    (b) Why does she not want to call out to her mother? **2 points**
    *   she does not want to pester her
    *   in case her mother has to leave her too

(20 points)

= 20 marks

6. Translate into English:

    „Das machen wir trotzdem . . . fest in den Arm genommen." (lines 12–15) **10**

(30)

Translation

'We'll still do it,'   he said, '(I) promise.'
'We'll do it nevertheless,'

And then he had left.
                    driven away.

Just as he did every morning
Like

as if he'd be back in a few hours.

Before he had got into the car he had held her tightly.
                        hugged

50

Passage 2

Ein Wochenende in der Provinz

1. Give details of any two free time activities on offer to teenagers in Anklam. **2 points**
    - the only youth club is open for a few hours on Tuesdays and Thursdays
    - only children use the small swimming pool
    - there is a film on in the theatre only two or three times a week
    (any 2)

2. The weekends can be very boring (lines 8–12).
    What does Conny vaguely remember doing last weekend? **2 points**
    - she spent the whole of Saturday in bed
    - and watched television

3. Read paragraph 3 (lines 13–18).

    (a) Why do the young unemployed look forward to the weekend? **1 point**
    - they meet up with loads of people of the same age

    (b) What are we told about *Onkel Ben*? **1 point**
    - it is the only pub in town young people find acceptable

    (c) What is usually the main topic of conversation? **1 point**
    - who is friends with whom and since when / for how long

4. Now read lines 19–27.

    (a) How does Conny intend spending the coming weekend? **1 point**
    - she is going to study (for her exams)
    OR
    - she has arranged to meet up with a friend to practise / go over their maths together

    (b) Mention two things she would normally do at the weekend. **2 points**
    - go to birthday parties
    - drive around the local area with her boyfriend, Kristian
    - in summer she has a barbecue with friends in the garden or at the lake
    (any 2)

5. Read the information about Kristian (lines 32–39).

    (a) Why does he go to bed at six o' clock on a Friday? **2 points**
    - he works from midnight until 9am
    - as an apprentice baker

    (b) Mention in detail three specific benefits of having a car in Anklam. **3 points**

- you can drive to surrounding towns and villages
- you can go to a different disco and meet other people
- in summer you can go swimming in the Baltic
- you can go shopping in Poland (which is nearby) where cigarettes are particularly cheap
  (any 3)

6. Now read the information about Kathrin and Mandy (lines 40–46).

    (a) Why does Kathrin have to work this Sunday?   **2 points**
    - it is Mother's Day
    - many people need a bunch of flowers

    (b) Why does Mandy not find reception work stressful?   **1 point**
    - in the last five hours no one has come in or phoned

7. In the last section (lines 54–56) we are told how things have changed for parents since the reunification of Germany. Mention two changes.   **2 points**
    - parents used to be less stressed at work and had time to go out at the weekend
    - today many parents work at the weekend because they have to or because it is worth it

                                                                        (20 points)

                                                                        = 20 marks

8. Translate into English:
    „Das ist wichtig ... und Bekannte besuchen."
    (lines 28–31)   **10**

                                                                        (30)

Translation

This is important because he has a driving licence,
                    for   can drive

(he has) a car and even his own flat.

Kristian uses his car practically every weekend to visit his mother who is seriously ill.

He takes her out for a run in the car,
                    drive

to go shopping and to visit friends.
for   acquaintances

Passage 4

Ich verlor meine Mutter – aber fand meinen Vater

1. In paragraph 1 we are told of Ingrid's fond memories of her mother. What does she remember? **2 points**
    - they did a lot of things together
    - they used to sing and dance to old Abba hits

2. Ingrid owes her happy childhood to her mother.

    (a) Why did she never know her father? **1 point**
    - her mother and father split up six months after her birth

    (b) What sort of things did she and her mother do together? **2 points**
    - they went to London for the weekend to go shopping or to go to a museum
    - they visited relations (relatives) afterwards
    - in the holidays they often went to the seaside
    (any 2)

3. In lines 11–19 we are told of the events which changed her life forever.

    (a) Why did Ingrid have to go to her grandmother's? **2 points**
    - her mother had to go to hospital
    - for a routine operation

    (b) What gave her reason for concern one week later? **1 point**
    - her mother had to be transferred to intensive care

    (c) What fact suggests that her mother's death was particularly tragic? **1 point**
    - she was only 38

4. Read paragraph 4 (lines 20–27)

    (a) What did she find out about the Salvation Army? **1 point**
    - they can help trace missing people

    (b) What was the one question which kept going through her head? **1 point**
    - what her father looked like today

5. Ingrid's grandmother was of help during this time (lines 28–42).

    (a) What was she told by the Salvation Army officers? **2 points**
    - it is sometimes very difficult to find someone
    - especially when all contact has been broken off for some time

(b)   When Kevin was finally found and Ingrid considered meeting him, which two
         thoughts went through her mind about him?   **2 points**
- he might have his own family / a new family
- he might not want to know anything about her

(c)   What did she ask her grandmother to do?   **1 point**
- arrange a meeting for her with her father

6.   Ingrid's reunion with her father was not as emotional as you might expect (lines 48–56).
      How did they react to each other before they exchanged information?   **2 points**
- all she could say was 'hello'
- there were no tears
- there was no heartfelt hug
- they were like strangers
  (any 2)

7.   What evidence is there in the final paragraph that her relationship with her father will
      continue to develop?   **2 points**
- they meet up nearly every weekend
- he often visits her at her gran's and she has already been twice
  to his house
- he has invited her to go to Cyprus with him this summer
- they are having a lot of fun getting to know each other
  (any 2)   **20 points**

                                                                                    = 20 marks

8.   Translate into English:
      „Als ich nach Hause kam . . . lang nicht gesehen hatte.“

      (lines 44–48)   **10**

                                                                                               (30)

Translation

When I came home I knew that he would be there

– there was no going back. Slowly I unlocked the door and went in.
                     turning
                     backing out

I heard voices (coming) from the living room.

Then I was standing in front of him – my father

Whom I had not seen in 16 years
 who   hadn't   for   **10**

                                                                                                30

Passage 4

Meine Mutter behandelte mich wie ein Kind

1. In lines 1–9 we are told why Hannelore's mother came to live with her.

   (a) What event prompted her mother to move in?   **1 point**
   - the death of Hannelore's father

   (b) Why did Hannelore think that her mother would have been better moving in with her
   other daughters?   **3 points**
   - the other two daughters got on much better with their mother
   - they are both married and live in large detached houses
   - they would have had more room to take her in
   - Hannelore only lived in a small, two-roomed flat
   (any 3)

   (c) What solution did her mother come up with?   **1 point**
   - she and Hannelore could rent a bigger flat

2. There were domestic problems right from the start. Mention two specific areas of friction.   **2 points**
   - her mother claimed she did not prepare the food properly / in
     the right way
   - only her mother could sort out the washing correctly
   - her mother found fault with the way Hannelore prepared the cat's food
   (any 2)

3. Read lines 19–25.

   (a) Domestic arrangements apart, how else did her mother interfere with her life?   **1 point**
   - she interfered in Hannelore's friendships

   (b) What did her mother do on a Saturday evening?   **2 points**
   - she stood behind the front door to catch / intercept her daughter's
     friend
   - she then interrogated him about his intentions towards her daughter

   (c) What effect did this have on most of the men?   **1 point**
   - they did not want to see Hannelore again

4. Read lines 33–43.

   (a) Where exactly did Hannelore meet Manfred?   **1 point**
   - at a colleague's birthday party

   (b) How do you know that they were attracted?   **2 points**
   - she spent the whole of the evening talking to him
   - they became close quickly

- they arranged to meet again the very next day
  (any 2)

(c)   Why did Manfred not fear meeting her mother?   **1 point**
- he always got on well with people

5.   Manfred finally meets her mother (lines 44–52).

(a)   How did he respond to her pointed remarks?   **1 point**
- he was not offended but found them funny

(b)   Despite her mother's initial reservations, how did she respond to Manfred once she
      got to know him?   **2 points**
- she started to like him
- they got on very well with each other

6.   Manfred helped her mother see her life differently (lines 53–59).

(a)   What conclusion did she draw?   **1 point**
- that she was wasting her time

(b)   Why did she finally leave her daughter alone?   **1 point**
- she became so involved in parish / church work

                                                                    (20 points)

                                                                    = 20 marks

7.   Translate into English:
     „Nach ihrer Abfahrt … wie ich wollte.“ (lines 30–32)   **10**

                                                                    (30)

Translation

After her departure I lived (my life) again as I pleased,
        she (had) left   I wanted

ate what I liked,

had a long lie-in on Saturday,
        sleep in

fed the cat from tins
                (with) tinned food

and went out at the weekend for as long as I wanted.

Passage 5

Mein Sohn ist ein Fixer

1. In lines 1–10 we are told about Evelyn Buchmann's sadness.

    (a) Why will she never forget her son's 30th birthday?   **1 point**
        - on that day she gave up the fight for her drug-addicted son
        OR
        - she gave up on her son and did not send him a birthday card or present

    (b) What showed her determination until this point and makes her defeat all the more tragic?   **2 points**
        - for 15 years she had tried to be stronger than hashish, heroin and methadone
        - for 5475 days she had believed she could break the vicious circle of drug-taking in which her son was involved

2. Read lines 11–14. What evidence is there that Evelyn Buchmann has not only been affected emotionally, but physically too?   **3 points**
        - she looks pale and tired
        - her eyes lack sparkle
        - her hands twitch / shake / flutter nervously
        - her energy and optimism have been destroyed
        (any 3)

3. Now read lines 15–20.

    (a) What was Evelyn's job?   **1 point**
        - manager of a small Swiss building contractor / construction firm

    (b) Why is she now reluctant to leave her flat?   **2 points**
        - she is afraid of meeting Daniel
        - she cannot bear seeing his rundown / impoverished existence (instead of leading a normal life)

4. Evelyn's home town of Aarau is described (lines 21–26).

    (a) In what way is its appearance misleading?   **2 points**
        - it appears to be very clean and respectable / orderly
        - it is actually contaminated with drug-related problems / drugs

    (b) How was Daniel's drug addiction dealt with 15 years ago?   **2 points**
        - there were no drug counselling facilities
        OR

 • there was no help available for drug addicts
 • the problem was swept under the carpet

5.   Evelyn's mother helped to bring up Daniel (lines 31–37).

   (a)   Why was this necessary?   **2 points**
            • Evelyn had to work
            • she did not have much money

   (b)   How was he treated by his grandmother?   **3 points**
              • he was completely spoiled
              • she regarded him as her property
              • he could do whatever he wanted with her
              • she never scolded him when he had behaved badly
                (any 3)

6.   Before Daniel ended up living on the street he found a job (lines 49–55).

   (a)   What did he work as?   **1 point**
            • he was an <u>apprentice</u> painter

   (b)   Why did he leave this job?   **1 point**
            • he fell out / argued / had an argument with his boss

                                                                   (20 points)

                                                                   = 20 marks

7.   Translate into English:
      „Mit fünfzehn Jahren wurde er ... konnte ich machen?"
      (lines 42–46).   **(10)**

                                                                   (30)

Translation

   "When he was fifteen he was caught smoking for the third time
         Aged

   and had to leave school.

   When I tried to talk to Daniel about it he became aggressive
                  talking

   and said that he didn't want to stay on any longer at school anyway.

   He didn't care.   What could I do?"
   He couldn't care less.
   It was all the same to him.

Passage 6

Das Dream-Team vom Traumschiff

1. In the opening paragraph what are we told about most of the passengers on board the *Caronia*?   **1 point**
    - they are pensioners

2. Why do most of the crew do this job for a limited time?   **2 points**
    - to escape boredom
    - to further their career

3. Read about Sibylle in paragraph 2 (lines 11–19).

    (a) As the official 'hostess' on board, mention two things her job involves.   **2 points**
    - she organises quiz shows
    - she accompanies guests on excursions ashore
    - she is on hand to give information
    (any 2)

    (b) What exactly are her working hours?   **2 points**
    - from 8.30am to about 1am
    OR
    - from 8.30am until the orchestra has finished playing

4. Read paragraph 3 (lines 20–25).
    How do Alexandra and her boyfriend spend their leave together?   **2 points**
    - they travel
    - they spend their time together in the flat they share

5. Read the information about Esther (lines 26–32).

    (a) What are her duties on board?   **2 points**
    - disposing of refuse
    - she is responsible for the crew accommodation

    (b) Mention two chores she does not miss having to do back home.   **2 points**
    - paying bills
    - washing clothes
    - shopping
    - cooking
    (any 2)

6. Read paragraph 5 (lines 33–41).

    (a) Why does Birgit consider her salary a good one?   **1 point**
    - there is practically nothing to spend your money on on board

59

(b)   Mention two things which annoy her on board.   **2 points**
  • constant repetition
  • the tiredness she feels keeping her balance behind the bar
  • the cabin she has to share with various room-mates
  • the difficulties in having a relationship
  (any 2)

7.   Read the information about Katrin (lines 42–53).

(a)   Why is her career as chef unusual for a woman?   **2 points**
  • she gives the orders to 35 men

(b)   Mention one drawback in this job.   **1 point**
  • she has to work a 12-hour day
  OR
  • she misses rock concerts and her friends

8.   In the final paragraph Oliver claims that each member of the crew is running away from problems.

  Mention one such problem.   **1 point**
  • from an unhappy love affair
  • from a marriage on the rocks
  • from a business collapse / bankruptcy
  (any 1)   **(20 points)**

                                                                                         = 20 marks

9.   Translate into English:
  „Nach ein paar Monaten ... waren zu deprimierend.“
  (lines 42–45).   **10**

                                                                                         (30)

Translation

After a few months on board

Katrin tried to work in Switzerland again

but in the end she came back to the ship.
                              on board

The bad pay ashore

and the lousy promotion prospects as a cook were too depressing.

Passage 7

Ein Semester fern der Heimat

1. How did Jean-Baptiste end up studying engineering for a semester in Bochum?   **2 points**
    - he received a European Union grant
    - Bochum university is twinned with Belfort university
      (his university in France), which organised the trip

2. Read paragraph 3 (lines 12–20).

    (a) What do Christian and Jean-Baptiste have in common?   **1 point**
    - they are both studying engineering

    (b) Why does the journey to his destination take longer than Jean-Baptiste expected?   **1 point**
    - the Ruhr University campus is situated outside the town
    OR
    - the halls of residence are outside the town

    (c) Why is this an advantage for people like Jean-Baptiste?   **1 point**
    - you can go jogging

3. Read the information about his accommodation (lines 21–33).

    (a) What does Jean-Baptiste find on his door?   **2 points**
    - three nameplates
    - a small German flag beside the names of his two room-mates

    (b) What two advantages are there for foreign students like Jean-Baptiste in living here?   **2 points**
    - living with Germans he will not only improve his language
    - he will get to know Germans straight away

    (c) What is his one disappointment?   **1 point**
    - his room-mates are not there
    OR
    - his room-mates are at their parents' home

4. Hanna and Christian take Jean-Baptiste to the students' pub (lines 34–39).
    What does he talk about with the German students?   **1 point**
    - the differences between studying / courses in France and in Germany
    OR
    - in France they have 35 hours tuition a week and only 20 in Germany

5. Read how Jean-Baptiste will spend his first three weeks (lines 40–47).

    (a) Apart from the language course, mention any two planned activities.   **2 points**
    - visits to the theatre

- evening concerts
- visits to cities such as Cologne and Essen
  (any 2)

(b) Mention two areas of study in his language course. **2 points**
- pronunciation practice
- listening comprehension
- reading skills
- everyday / general conversation
  (any 2)

(c) In which area did he make most progress? **1 point**
- (he broadened his) vocabulary

6. Read the information about the student refectory (lines 48–52).
   Mention two things which impress Jean-Baptiste. **2 points**
- the choice and quality of the food
- the fact that provision is made for vegetarians

7. Read the last two paragraphs (lines 53–64).

(a) What do Jean-Baptiste and the two Spanish girls find out from the locals? **1 point**
- the pub district in Bochum is called the *Bermuda Triangle*

(b) Why is it important for Jean-Baptiste to sort out his course with his adviser of studies? **1 point**
- so that his semester in Bochum will be recognised by his own
  university

(20 points)

= 20 marks

8. Translate into English:
   „Jean-Baptiste steigt aus ... Telefonnummer bekommen.“
   (lines 5–8) **10**

(30)

Translation

Jean-Baptiste gets out of the Intercity express.

He is carrying a heavy travelling bag.
case

A guitar hangs over his shoulder.

He looks for a phone and calls Hanna.

He got her telephone number before he left.
set off

his departure

Passage 8

Ferienjobs für Studenten

1. Mention three advantages of working in the holidays. **3 points**
    - you can use the experience as a springboard towards a future career
    OR
    - it is good experience for a future career

    - you can work in attractive holiday locations / areas
    - you can brush up or broaden your languages
    - you can gain interesting insights into the everyday life and culture of another country
    (any 3)

2. Why is it important to organise your job in good time? **1 point**
    - the best offers are quickly taken

3. Now read the information about Sabine (lines 11–20).

    (a) How did she get her job on Fuerteventura? **1 point**
    - she simply asked at a local club there

    (b) Mention two things her work involved during the day. **2 points**
    - organising hikes / walks
    - giving language lessons
    - taking part in beach gymnastics
    (any 2)

4. Now read the information about Claudia (lines 21–29).

    (a) Where exactly does she work? **1 point**
    - in a vegetarian restaurant (in Bonn)

    (b) Mention two things her work involves. **2 points**
    - setting tables
    - planning the various dishes
    - cashing up
    (any 2)

    (c) What are we told about the food on offer? **1 point**
    - it is incredibly varied
    OR
    - there is something different every day

    (d) What is the big advantage in working here? **1 point**
    - she can take home any leftovers / food that is left over

5. Now read about Thomas's job (lines 30–38).

    (a) What does he work as? **1 point**
    - he is a tourist guide

    (b) What did he learn on his training? **2 points**
    - the history of the town
    - history of art

    (c) How is he often thanked for his work? **1 point**
    - he is invited out to stylish restaurants

6. Now read the information about Sonja (lines 39–50).

    (a) Why is she particularly suited to this kind of work? **1 point**
    - she is bilingual

    OR
    - she is very interested in languages

    (b) Why does she not accept the full-time job offers? **1 point**
    - she wants to finish her studies first

7. Now read the tips given (lines 51–61).

    (a) Why are those working abroad advised to see a doctor? **1 point**
    - they may need certain medicine or vaccinations

    (b) What must you do before you go back to your everyday routine? **1 point**
    - have a little holiday / relaxation **(20 points)**

                                                               = 20 marks

8. Translate into English:
    „Nachdem ich mein Studium ... bei einer Fluggesellschaft."
    (lines 17–20).   **10**

                                                                  (30)

Translation

After I had finished my studies in Germany

I went back and stayed for a few more years.
My time   on the island was the best I had ever had

The time I spent

and I was lucky: due to   my experience
          fortunate   because of
                       owing to

I found a job with an airline company.

Passage 9

Lust auf Zukunft

1. Read the information about Annette in paragraph 1 (lines 1–14).

   (a) Where was she when she should have been at school?   **2 points**
- at the cinema or in town
- at her best friend's house

   (b) What was the consequence of this?   **2 points**
- her marks became worse
- she had to leave school at 16

   (c) In what way did Sven have a positive influence on her education?   **1 point**
- he made her attend classes / lessons

   (d) Mention two courses of study offered at Annette's college.   **2 points**
- painter and varnisher
- domestic science (home economics)
- personal hygiene
(any 2)

2. Read lines 15–24.

   (a) Why was Annette lucky to be given the chance to work for the *Hauptschule* exams?   **1 point**
- few are allowed to do this

   (b) What does this tell us about her work at the college?   **1 point**
- her class participation showed promise

   (c) Why did Annette never skip classes here?   **2 points**
- it was much more fun (than school)
- she did not want to spoil her future

3. Read paragraphs 3 and 4 (lines 25–40).

   (a) Why did Manuel leave school?   **2 points**
- his marks were not very good
- he found studying German and Maths particularly hard

   (b) Why did he not enjoy his free time when he worked in the supermarket?   **2 points**
- he had too much free time
- his friends worked all day and did not have much time for him
- it was really boring (he was bored)
(any 2)

(c)   What was his parents' attitude towards his career?   **1 point**
- they did not get involved

OR
- they said his job was his concern alone

4.   Now read lines 43–52.

(a)   What did Manuel realise after his first placement in a business?   **1 point**
- an 8-hour-a-day office job was not for him

(b)   Mention one advantage of working as a retailer.   **1 point**
- he is not always sitting in an office

OR
- the working hours are more flexible

5.   Now read the information about Jochen (lines 53–62).

(a)   Why does he like working with metal?   **1 point**
- he gets to work outside

(b)   Mention one typical task in his line of work.   **1 point**
- putting up bus stops

OR
- putting in / installing window frames at building sites   **(20 points)**

     = 20 marks

6.   Translate into English:

„In diesem Beruf … nicht in Sicht." (lines 39–43)   **10**

     (30)

Translation

In this job   his foreign languages are useful.
     profession   knowledge of foreign languages is useful

The interviews at   various companies went well according to
     with   different

Manuel.

Nevertheless he did not get a job:
Yet
But

"Perhaps my marks were too bad."
     grades

Suddenly Manuel was 20 and a job was not in sight.
     there was no job on the horizon

Passage 10

Warten auf den blauen Brief

1. Read lines 1–18.

    (a)   How did Clara respond when she got a 'six' for the first time?   **1 point**
- she howled / cried the whole afternoon

    (b)   How did Clara manage to bluff her way through in the 'fifth year'?   **2 points**
- she learned a little vocabulary
- she revised some more before the class test

    (c)   Why did she not spend much time swotting up her grammar?   **2 points**
- she found it much too complicated
- she hated it

    (d)   Why does she think it would be unfair for her to repeat the whole year?   **2 points**
- she is not that bad in school
- in Maths she even gets good marks

2. Clara considers the consequences of having to repeat a whole year (lines 19–29).

    (a)   Mention two things which she will have to do again.   **2 points**
- plants and animals in Biology
- in German an essay on the same topic as last year's

    (b)   Why will she be particularly disappointed not to study English?   **2 points**
- her friends will have the chance to go on an exchange trip to England
- and she had been so looking forward to this

    (c)   What reservations does she have about being in classes with younger pupils?   **2 points**
- they will be childish
- she is already one year older
- they will think that she is hopeless
- they may not want to have anything to do with her
  (any 2)

3. Read lines 30–35.

    What is Clara most afraid of?   **2 points**
- that her friends will not like her (because she is having to repeat a year)
- that they will lose touch / they will stop seeing each other / it will be difficult to keep the friendships

4. Clara mentions her family (lines 39–50).

    (a)   Why is her mother perhaps glad that she might have to repeat the year?   **1 point**
        • Clara will not be spending so much time with her friends

    (b)   How was she punished after the second piece of Latin homework?   **1 point**
        • Clara was grounded / she was not allowed to go out with her friends in the evening

    (c)   What action did her parents take to improve her grades?   **1 point**
        • her parents ordered her brother to help her
        OR
        • they paid for a tutor

5. Clara mentions her Latin teacher (lines 51–56).

    (a)   What exactly does she say about him?   **1 point**
        • he is a dreadful guy
        OR
        • he does not like her

    (b)   How did she respond when he humiliated her?   **1 point**
        • she went bright red / scarlet / as red as a beetroot

                  (20 points)

                  = 20 marks

6. Translate into English:
    „Meine Eltern wissen … mein Zeugnis vorbereitet."
    (lines 36–39)   **10**

                  (30)

Translation

My parents know that I may have to repeat the year.

They are really understanding and we don't argue about it at home.
                quarrel

I think I owe this to my form teacher.
    I have my form teacher to thank for this

She had a chat with my mother
    talked to

and prepared her for my report.

Passage 11

Eine schrecklich nette Familie

1. Which question is a favourite with interviewers?   **1 point**
    - what would you most like to take with you to a desert island?

2. Mention two kinds of holiday we might spend with our friends.   **2 points**
    - we rent a cottage / little house in Corfu
    - we rent a flat / apartment in Majorca
    - we go yachting in the Mediterranean
      (any 2)

3. In paragraph 2 some of the advantages of going on holiday with friends are listed.

    (a)   What financial benefit is mentioned?   **1 point**
    - it is cheaper (and cosier) than in a hotel

    (b)   What advantage is there for an only child?   **1 point**
    - he/she gets to experience being part of a large family

4. Read lines 17–21.
    Mention two things Rolf intends doing with his friend.   **2 points**
    - sitting in the shade and smoking pipes
    - playing chess or writing a book

5. There is friction from the start (lines 22–28).

    (a)   How do we know that Rolf and Evelyne do not speak French very well?   **1 point**
    - they have to gesticulate to find out the way to the holiday house
      (they have to use their hands and feet to communicate)

    (b)   Give two reasons for Claudia's discontent.   **2 points**
    - she would much rather have had the big bedroom with the view
      than the small one to the back
    - she has been a vegetarian for two months and would prefer not to
      see any meat in the fridge

6. Claudia has invited some guests (lines 29–39).

    (a)   Why does Gran not want a dog in the house?   **1 point**
    - she is allergic to animal hairs

    (b)   Why is Evelyne annoyed that Claudia has invited Karen and Christian?   **1 point**
- she and her husband cannot stand them and Claudia knows this

7.   No one wants to wash up (lines 40–49).

    (a)   According to his wife, what is the real reason for Linus's bad mood?   **1 point**
- he has to lose weight and is not allowed to drink beer

    (b)   Why does Evelyne not want to wash up?   **1 point**
- she is allergic to washing-up liquid

    (c)   Why is Gran feeling unwell?   **2 points**
- too much garlic in the cooking
- she is not used to eating so late
- she has been sleeping badly
(any 2)

8.   Read lines 50–56.

    Why does Florian want to go home?   **2 points**
- he cannot stand the other children
- he hates having sailing lessons in French
- he hates visiting museums
- he wants his computer and to see his friends from the skateboard jump
(any 2)

9.   In the final paragraph the holidaymakers are considering next year's trips.

    Mention two of their plans.   **2 points**
- Evelyne and Rolf might go camping with the children
- Linus and Wibke want to take the children on a bike tour through Holland
- Claudia wants to go to Greece on her own in the hope of finding a new partner
- her son can visit his father
- Gran wants to stay at home and read magazines on her balcony
(any 2)   **20 points**

    = 20 marks

10.   Translate into English:

    „Sechs Erwachsene ... Computerbüchern."

    (lines 12–17)   **10**

    (30)

Translation

    Six adults and five children go to a wonderful, roomy holiday house
                                 travel

(which is) situated between (the) sea and (the) mountains in the south of France.

Evelyn would like most of all to lie in the sun, play tennis
Most of all   sunbathe
Above all else

and visit flea markets in remote villages.

Her husband, Rolf, normally likes staying in bed with piles of American computer books.

Passage 12

Glasgow – eine freundliche Stadt

1. The journalist mentions two areas of Glasgow.
    How do they contrast? **2 points**
    - the Victorian architecture in the city centre is fabulous
    - the high-rise flats on the outskirts are dreadful

2. How does a Glaswegian respond when he is told that Glasgow has the reputation of being a 'tough' city? **2 points**
    - he says he has lived here all his life
    - and has experienced two fights at the most
    OR
    - he accepts there is violence
    - but says that there is violence everywhere

3. The journalist gives his own reason for this reputation.
    What comment does he make? **2 points**
    - violence is more dramatic than when nothing happens
    - so it makes good news / a good story

4. In paragraph 3 (lines 13–22), the journalist recounts an experience he had.

    (a) What brought the journalist and his colleagues to the South Side of the city? **2 points**
    - they wanted to take a few photographs
    - they needed panoramic views of the city centre for a piece in the "Herald"
    - they thought they would be able to take great pictures from the 16th floor of a high-rise block
    (any 2)

    (b) What are the two boys doing at the lift? **1 point**
    - they are playing headers with a tennis ball

    (c) How does one of the elderly women make the boys stop? **1 point**
    - she threatens to tell their mother

5. Unable to gain access to the roof, the journalist and his colleagues are given another opportunity (lines 28–47).

    (a) What does the young woman invite them to do? **1 point**
    - take photos from her balcony

    (b) Why is this successful? **1 point**
    - from there they have a great view of the town centre, the river and the many parks

72

    (c)   Mention two of the topics of conversation over tea and biscuits.   **2 points**
- the dreadful neighbours 'upstairs'
- life in high-rise flats
- how the family is
- the daughter's trip to see her sister in Canada
- how the sister in Canada is
  (any 2)

    (d)   What does the mother say when the men are leaving?   **1 point**
- they are to come back the next time they are in the area

6.   The journalist mentions a man he once met on Great Western Road (lines 48–58).

    (a)   How was the journalist feeling at the time?   **1 point**
- very depressed

    (b)   Why did the stranger not want to go home?   **2 points**
- he had been out clubbing and drinking with a friend
- he hadn't been home for a few nights to see his wife and three children

    (c)   Which two options was the stranger contemplating?   **1 point**
- going straight home or going out for another night on the town

7.   In the final paragraph, how does the journalist describe Glasgow?   **1 point**
- a city in which it is hard to feel lonely

    (20 points)

    = 20 marks

8.   Translate into English:
    ,,Auf dem Weg ... draußen gibt." (lines 23–26)   **10**

    (30)

Translation

On the way up in the lift everyone gradually gets off,

apart from the young woman and the three of us.

We speak to her and explain why we are here.

We would like to get (out) onto the roof.

She says that on the top floor there is an outside door.

Passage 13

Sprachkurs

1. Read the paragraph about Julia (lines 1–13).

    (a) Why did Julia and her friend feel forced to learn English?   **1 point**
    - to get to know people on the beach

    (b) Why was the revision of grammar not so important for her?   **1 point**
    - she always got good marks for her written work in school

    (c) Why was a meeting before the trip helpful?   **2 points**
    - they were given information about the lessons / classes
    - they were given good tips on planning the trip

    (d) What would she pay particular attention to next time?   **1 point**
    - that she does not have to share accommodation with other Germans

    (e) What reason does she give for this?   **1 point**
    - you are forced to speak more English

2. Now read the section on Daniel (lines 14–29).

    (a) Give details of the first problem he encountered on the island.   **2 points**
    - Germans were walking around everywhere;
    - in the language schools, in the guesthouses
    - and in the youth hostel in which he stayed
      (any 2)

    (b) Why was the weather a problem too?   **2 points**
    - in temperatures of around 40 degrees
    - it was impossible to concentrate

3. Now read Dieter's account (lines 30–42).

    (a) Why did he go to England?   **1 point**
    - to get rid of his language inhibitions

    (b) Why were the lessons boring?   **2 points**
    - they swotted up grammar the whole time
    - there was much too little English spoken
    - the whole lesson was dominated by three people
      (any 2)

    (c) What comment does he make about the host parents?   **1 point**
    - they showed no interest beyond asking: 'What did you do today?'

4. Now read about Saskia's experience (lines 43–53).

   (a) What positive effect did Saskia's stay have on her English?   **2 points**
- she enjoys the lessons more now
- she has become more confident in speaking
- she participates more
  (any 2)

   (b) In what way were her teacher's lessons effective?   **1 point**
- no one could avoid speaking

OR
- everyone had to speak

5. A few tips are given for prospective students (lines 54–61).

   (a) Why is it important to have someone you can contact at any time while you are at the school?   **1 point**
- in case you are unhappy with the course or any other problems arise

   (b) What information will be in the contract?   **2 points**
- the number of lessons there are a day
- what the accommodation is like
- what free time activities are on offer
  (any 2)   **(20 points)**

   = 20 marks

6. Translate into English:
„Unsere Lehrer waren ... Deutsch geredet."
(lines 20–24)   **10**

   (30)

Translation

Our teachers were local students

whose pronunciation was even worse than ours.
     accent

We learned absolutely nothing in the lessons:
              class

of the one and a half hours daily of grammar
there were no written exercises

and in the conversation classes we mainly spoke German.
          predominantly

DIRECTED WRITING

ADVICE TO CANDIDATES

- Read through the whole scenario carefully. It is imperative that you include all the information correctly and that you make reference to each bullet point. Some bullet points may require you to give more than one piece of information.

- Tick off each bullet point once you have written down the appropriate information. You may find that in the first two bullet points you are able to include all the relevant information in just a couple of lines.

- Always refer back to the scenario in the introduction. It is important that you give the correct information, e.g. if it is specified that you went to Germany last summer for two weeks, you must convey this information exactly, or if it states that you travelled by bus and ferry, you must not write that you flew from Glasgow Prestwick!

- Remember too that you are encouraged to give 'any other relevant details'. This is your opportunity to show off the German you know and to incorporate any relevant expressions you have learned during the year.

- Restrict your use of a dictionary to looking up key words required to convey the message in any of the bullet points or in the scenario. e.g. a choir, a restaurant, a concert, to go camping, etc., and for checking the spellings and genders of what you have already written.

- Give your writing some structure. Make sure you put in an introduction to set the scene (based on part of the scenario and perhaps the first couple of bullet points), develop your account in two or three paragraphs (stick closely to the bullet points but develop your ideas to show off the German you know), and in the final paragraph draw the piece of writing to a conclusion (sum up the whole experience and refer to the last bullet point).

- There is no advantage in exceeding the word limit. Provided you have included all the points accurately, credit will be given.

- Time yourself. Make sure you can complete the task in 40 minutes.

- Check all grammar – particularly verbs and word order.

(1) Verbs

You will probably have used the perfect tense to convey what happened in the past. Check to see you have used the correct part of the correct auxiliary verb, i.e. *sein* or *haben*, e.g. *ich <u>bin</u> ... gegangen*, *wir <u>haben</u> ... besucht*, etc.

(2) Word Order

*   The verb must be the second 'item', e.g. *ich <u>fuhr</u> letztes Jahr nach Deutschland.*
        1st 2nd

*   Remember to keep the verb as the second 'item' if the subject does not come first, e.g.
    <u>letztes Jahr</u> <u>fuhr</u> ich nach Deutschland.
        1st   2nd

*   ***Time-Manner-Place*** rule. Expressions of time, manner and place must fall in that order
    – time before manner before place:
    e.g. *<u>Letzten Sommer</u> fuhr ich <u>mit dem Zug</u> <u>nach Deutschland</u>.*
        time   manner   place

*   ***Subordinating clauses***
    Have you used any subordinating conjunctions, i.e. words like *weil* (because), *als* (when), *wenn* (whenever / if), *dass* (that), *obwohl* (although), etc. Make sure that the verb is placed at the end of the clause, e.g. *Wir haben viel unternommen,* **obwohl** *das Wetter schlecht <u>war</u>,* or *ich habe mich total gelangweilt,* **weil** *meine Eltern nur in Museen gehen <u>wollten</u>.*

*   ***Co-ordinating conjunctions***
    Remember that the following words do <u>not</u> change word order: *und* (and), *oder* (or), *aber* (but), *sondern* (but – to contradict a negative statement) and *denn* (for – in the sense 'because').

THE MARKING OF THE DIRECTED WRITING

You are awarded a pegged mark out of 15 for this paper. A very good piece of writing will be awarded 15 / 15, a good piece of writing will be awarded 12 / 15, a satisfactory effort will be awarded 9 / 15, an unsatisfactory attempt will be given 6 / 15, a poor piece of work will be awarded 3 / 15 and a very poor attempt will be given no marks. For every bullet point omitted, two raw marks will be deducted. (Therefore, if you produce a 'good' piece of writing – 12 / 15 – but omit 1 bullet point your final score will be 10 / 15. If you miss out three or more bullet points you will be awarded no marks.)

To score highly in this paper you need to demonstrate a high level of accuracy, communicate clearly throughout and include all the information that is required. My advice is to practise writing as many different scenarios as possible during the year, paying close attention to the mistakes that you are making so that they do not recur in a subsequent piece of writing. On the day of the examination include all the bullet points, but write only what you know to be correct.

DIRECTED WRITING 1

Last summer you worked in Germany for two months before going to university. Towards the end of your stay you met a young German person who was considering finding a summer job in Britain.

On your return, you write to him / her, **in German**, to tell him / her of your experiences.

You must include the following information and **you should try to add** other relevant details:

- where you stayed in Germany and for how long

- where you worked and what you thought of the job

- the hours you worked and how you got on with your boss

- how you spent your free time

- any aspects of your stay you did not enjoy

- whether you would recommend working abroad

Your account should be 150–180 words in length. (15)

DIRECTED WRITING 2

Last Easter you spent a fortnight with your pen-friend in Germany. You travelled there by train and by boat. You spent one week at his / her home. During this time you met all of his / her friends. The second week you went camping with your pen-friend and his / her family.

Now you have been asked to write an account of your experiences **in German** for inclusion in the foreign language section of your school / college magazine.

You must include the following information and **you should try to add** other relevant details:

- how you travelled to Germany and what you did during the journey

- who was in his / her family and how you got on with them

- what your pen-friend's home was like

- what you did with your pen-friend the first week

- whether you enjoyed the camping trip

- whether you would go back to stay with them again

Your account should be 150–180 words in length. (15)

DIRECTED WRITING 3

Last June a group of Austrian pupils / students came to your school / college on an exchange trip for 10 days. One of them stayed with you. The Austrian students spent one day in your school / college.

You have been chosen to write a report of the trip, **in German**, to send to the exchange school / college.

You must include the following information and **you should try to add** other relevant details:

- who stayed with you and for how long

- what the Austrian person thought of your home

- what he / she thought of your school / college

- what else you did together during his / her stay

  what he / she disliked about Scotland

  whether you plan to visit him / her in Austria

  count should be 150–180 words in length.   **(15)**

DIRECTED WRITING 4

Last summer a Swiss choir came to stay and to perform in your town for three days. Your family offered to host two of the choir members. As you are the only German speaker in the family, you agreed to help out, to go with them to some concerts in the evening and to show them the sights in your town in the afternoon.

ou have been asked by the choirmaster to write a report, **in German**, for his community gazine.

must include the following information and **you should try to add** other relevant details:

vho exactly came to stay and for how long

hat they thought of Scottish food

hat you did with them in the afternoons

hat you thought of their concerts

ou enjoyed their stay

ether you would play host again

count should be 150–180 words in length. (15)

DIRECTED WRITING 5

Last October you went on a school trip to Koblenz for five days. You travelled via Belgium by coach and overnight ferry with six teachers and 47 of your classmates. You stayed in a youth hostel in the centre of the city. One day you went on an excursion to the city of Cologne to visit the cathedral.

On your return you are asked to write a report of your trip, **in German**, for inclusion in the school magazine.

You must include the following information and **you should try to add** other relevant details

- who went on the trip and how long you were away

- how you travelled and what you did during the journey

- where you stayed and what you thought of the accommodation

- what you did during your stay

- how you got on with your friends and teachers

- whether you would go on a school trip in the future

Your account should be 150–180 words in length.

DIRECTED WRITING 6

Last year you went to Vienna to study in a German speaking school / college. You shared a flat with three other gap students. You attended school / college every day and at the weekends and holidays you went travelling with your flatmates.

On your return you are asked to write a report, **in German**, of your year abroad for the Austrian school magazine.

You must include the following information and **you should try to add** other relevant details:

* where you stayed and with whom you shared

* which subjects you studied

* how this school compared with your own school / college

* how you organised the cooking and the housework in your flat

* what you did at weekends and during the holidays

* if you would recommend a year abroad to prospective students

Your account should be 150–180 words in length. (15)

DIRECTED WRITING 7

Last summer you went on a family holiday. Your family rented a cottage in the Baltic Sea resort of Ostseebad Boltenhagen and you spent three weeks there. During your stay you met others of the same age and spent some time with them. During the day you went to the beach with your family or went shopping, and in the evening you went out with your friends.

Now you have been asked to write about your experiences, **in German**, for your German class.

You must include the following information and **you should try to add** other relevant details:

* with whom you went and how long you stayed

* where you stayed and what you thought of the accommodation

* what you did to help your family with the housework

* what you did during the day

* what you did with your friends in the evening

* whether you would like to go on holiday with your family again

Your account should be 150–180 words in length.   (15)

DIRECTED WRITING 8

Last winter you went on a school skiing trip to Garmisch-Partenkirchen in the German Alps for a week. You flew to Munich and then took a coach to your hotel. You travelled with 19 other pupils and four teachers. You went skiing during the day, although the weather was bad. In the evening you went out with your friends in the village.

On your return, you are asked to write about the trip, **in German**, for your school magazine.

You must include the following information and **you should try to add** other relevant details:

*   where exactly you went and who went with you

*   where you stayed and with whom you shared a room

*   what the weather was like

*   what you did during your stay

*   how you spent the evenings

*   if you would recommend a school skiing trip to other pupils

Your account should be 150–180 words in length.   **(15)**

DIRECTED WRITING 9

Last Easter you travelled alone to Germany to visit a Scottish friend who was studying at Trier university. You flew to Frankfurt and then took the train to the town of Trier. Your friend was ill while you were there and you had to go sightseeing on your own. On your return journey your flight was delayed for four hours.

Now you are writing to a German friend, **in German**, to tell him / her about your trip.

You must include the following information and **you should try to add** other relevant details:

* why you went to Germany and how you travelled

* what sightseeing you did during your stay in Trier

* what you did to help your friend

* if you enjoyed spending so much time on your own

* what you did at the airport on your return journey

* what you learned from the whole experience

Your account should be 150–180 words in length. (15)

DIRECTED WRITING 10

Last Christmas you and a friend organised a party for a group of Austrian pupils / students who had been on an exchange trip to your school. It was the last night of the Austrians' stay in Scotland.

You are asked to write a report about the evening, **in German**, for the school magazine.

You must include the following information and **you should try to add** other relevant details:

- where the party took place and how many people you invited

- what you and your friend did to organise it

- what you wore to the party

- how the evening went

- if you and your friend enjoyed the party

- what you did to tidy up after the party was over

Your account should be 150–180 words in length. (15)

DIRECTED WRITING PHRASES

Each of the following phrases relates directly to the bullet points in the Directed Writing tasks in this book. If you are having difficulty in expressing the message required in one of the bullet points, you will find an example of an appropriate phrase under the following headings:

- ☆ expressing when you went
- ☆ expressing why you went
- ☆ expressing where you went and with whom / who came to stay
- ☆ expressing how you travelled
- ☆ expressing what you did during the journey
- ☆ expressing how long you stayed
- ☆ expressing where you / they stayed
- ☆ describing your accommodation
- ☆ expressing how you got on with people
- ☆ giving your general opinion of your stay
- ☆ expressing what you did
- ☆ expressing likes and dislikes
- ☆ suggesting whether or not you would repeat the experience
- ☆ giving a reason for your opinion
- ☆ describing the job you did
- ☆ describing the weather

These phrases are not a substitute for learning the grammar rules, but they will provide emergency help if you are working alone on these papers. Of course, once you use any of the phrases you need to learn it so that if you are required to write something similar in the future, you will know the expression.

In the initial stages of Directed Writing, you may need to refer to a lot of these phrases and integrate them into your own German. As the Higher year progresses, however, and you learn many of the expressions and become more confident in German, you should become less dependent on this section of the book.

DIRECTED WRITING PHRASES

The following phrases relate directly to the Directed Writing topics in this book and should help you to write your essay.

Expressing when you went

letzten Sommer	last summer
letzten Winter	last winter
letztes Jahr	last year
in den Weihnachtsferien / Osterferien	in the Christmas / Easter holidays
vor zwei Jahren	two years ago
letzten Juni / Oktober	last June / October
letzte Weihnachten	last Christmas
letzte Ostern	last Easter

Expressing why you went

um meine Deutschsprachkenntnisse zu verbessern	to improve my Geman
bevor ich auf die Universität gegangen bin	before going to university
um einen Freund / eine Freundin zu besuchen	to visit a friend
um Geld zu verdienen	to earn money
ein Freund / eine Freundin von mir studierte an der Universität dort	a friend of mine was studying at the university there

Expressing where you went and with whom / who came to stay

ich bin nach Deutschland gefahren	I went to Germany
wir sind nach Österreich gefahren	we went to Austria
wir sind nach Köln gereist	we travelled to Cologne
ich habe in einem kleinen Dorf gewohnt	I stayed in a small village
ich habe ein Jahr an einer Schule in Wien verbracht	I spent one year at a school in Vienna
ich habe zwei Wochen mit meinen Eltern in einem Ferienort an der Ostsee verbracht	I spent two weeks with my parents in a holiday resort on the Baltic
zwölf Austauschschüler waren zu Besuch in unserer Schule	12 exchange pupils visited our school
ich bin mit meiner Familie weggefahren	I went away with my family
wir haben eine Pauschalreise gemacht	we went on a package holiday
ich habe eine Klassenfahrt gemacht	I went on a school trip
ich bin allein gereist	I travelled on my own
zwanzig Leute waren in der Gruppe	there were 20 people in the group
wir haben ein Häuschen an der Ostseeküste gemietet	we rented a cottage on the Baltic coast
wir sind in den Alpen Ski gefahren	we went skiing in the Alps
ein Mädchen hat bei mir gewohnt	a girl stayed with me
ein deutscher Junge ist zu mir zu Besuch gekommen	a German boy came to stay with me
zwei Jungen / Mädchen von dem Chor haben bei mir gewohnt	two boys / girls from the choir stayed with me

Expressing how you travelled

wir sind mit dem Zug gefahren 　　　　　　　Reisebus	we travelled by train 　　　　　　　　by coach
wir sind mit der Fähre von Hull nach Zeebrugge gefahren	we took the ferry from Hull to Zeebrugge
wir sind mit dem Flugzeug nach München gefflogen	we went by plane to Munich
ich habe den Zug und die Fähre genommen	I took the train and the ferry
ich bin von Glasgow nach Frankfurt geflogen	I flew from Glasgow to Frankfurt
der Flug hat anderthalb Stunden gedauert	the flight lasted an hour and a half
wir haben ein Auto am Flughafen gemietet	we rented a car at the airport

Expressing what you did during the journey

während der Reise bin ich eingeschlafen	during the journey I fell asleep
ich habe mich mit anderen Reisenden unterhalten	I talked to other travellers
ich habe aus dem Fenster geschaut	I looked out of the window
während der Reise habe ich die ganze Zeit gelesen	I read throughout the whole journey
am Flughafen habe ich auf mein Gepäck aufgepasst	at the airport I kept an eye on my luggage

Expressing how long you stayed

ich habe eine Woche in Köln verbracht	I spent one week in Cologne
wir haben zwei Wochen in Deutschland verbracht	we spent a fortnight in Germany
ich habe zwei Monate in einem Hotel in Deutschland gearbeitet	I worked for two months in an hotel in Germany
ich habe zwei Wochen dort verbracht	I spent a fortnight there

Expressing where you / they stayed

wir haben in einem schönen Hotel gewohnt	we stayed in a nice hotel
das Hotel befand sich in einem Wintersportort in den Alpen	the hotel was situated in a ski resort in the Alps
wir haben in einer Jugendherberge gewohnt	we stayed in a youth hostel
ich habe bei einer deutschen Familie gewohnt	I stayed with a German family
ich besuchte meinen Brieffreund / meine Brieffreundin	I visited my pen-friend
es waren vier in der Familie	there were four people in the family
wir haben auf dem Land gezeltet	we went camping in the country
wir haben auf einem Campingplatz gezeltet	we went camping at a campsite
ein Österreicher / eine Österreicherin hat bei mir gewohnt	an Austrian stayed with me

Describing your accommodation

er / sie wohnte in einem großen Einfamilienhaus	he / she lived in a large detached house
sein / ihr Haus war fabelhaft	his / her house was fabulous
das Hotel war hässlich	the hotel was ugly
die Wohnung war winzig	the flat was tiny
ich habe ein Zimmer mit einem Freund / einer Freundin geteilt	I shared a room with a friend
es gab ein beheiztes Schwimmbad, einen Fitnessraum und Satellitenfernsehen	there was a heated pool, a fitness room and satellite TV
der Campingplatz war sauber	the campsite was clean
der Waschraum war kalt und schmutzig	the wash block was cold and dirty
der SB-Laden war teuer	the self-service shop was expensive

es gab ein schönes Freibad	there was a nice open-air pool
der Campingplatz war modern ausgestattet	the campsite was fitted with modern equipment
meine Unterkunft war schrecklich	my accommodation was dreadful

Expressing how you got on with people

ich habe mich sehr gut mit der Familie verstanden	I got on really well with the family
mit meinem Chef / meiner Chefin	with my boss
mit seinen Freunden	with his friends
mit ihren Freunden	with her friends
mit meinen Lehrern	with my teachers
ich kam nicht sehr gut mit seinem Bruder aus	I did not get on very well with his brother
ich kam nicht gut mit ihrer Schwester aus	I did not get on well with her sister
ich habe viele nette Leute kennen gelernt	I met a lot of nice people
mein Chef / meine Chefin war sehr freundlich	my boss was very friendly

Giving your general opinion of your stay

es hat mir viel Spaß gemacht	I really enjoyed myself
wir haben uns sehr gut amüsiert	we had great fun
ich habe mich ein bisschen gelangweilt	I got a bit bored
ich hatte Heimweh	I felt homesick
meine Familie / meinen Hund habe ich vermisst	I missed my family / dog

Expressing what you did

ich bin einkaufen gegangen	I went shopping
wir haben beschlossen, eine Party zu machen / organisieren	we decided to have / organise a party
ich habe viele gleichaltrige Leute kennen gelernt	I met a lot of people of the same age
eines Abends sind wir in die Disko gegangen	we went clubbing one night
ich habe einen Einkaufsbummel gemacht	I went on a shopping spree
ich habe mich im Stadtzentrum verlaufen	I got lost in the town centre
am ersten Tag kam er zu meiner Schule	the first day he came to my school
ich bin häufig in Cafés gegangen	I often went to cafes
normalerweise bin ich um Mitternacht ins Bett gegangen	I normally went to bed at midnight
er hat oft Freunde zu sich nach Hause eingeladen	he often invited friends round
wir haben in der Jugendherberge zu Abend gegessen	we had our evening meal in the youth hostel
am Nachmittag habe ich entspannt	in the afternoon I relaxed
morgens habe ich mich am Strand gesonnt	in the morning I sunbathed on the beach
ich bin mit meiner Familie zum Strand gegangen	I went to the beach with my family
wir sind zusammen essen gegangen	we went out for a meal together
ich bin in ein paar Konzerte gegangen	I went to a few concerts
abends sind wir ins Kino gegangen	we went to the cinema in the evening
wir haben versucht, mit den Einheimischen zu reden	we tried to speak to the locals
wir haben alle Sehenswürdigkeiten besichtigt	we visited all the sights
ich habe einen Tagesausflug nach Köln gemacht	I went on a day trip to Cologne

ich habe die Wohnung sauber gemacht	I cleaned the flat
jeden Morgen staubsaugte ich	every morning I did the vacuum cleaning
am Abend habe ich meiner Mutter geholfen, das Abendessen vorzubereiten	in the evening I helped my mother prepare the meal
wir haben tolle Ausflüge gemacht	we went on great outings
wir haben so viel unternommen	we did so much
wir haben Wanderungen im Gebirge gemacht	we went hiking in the mountains
wir sind Wasserski laufen gegangen	we went water skiing
wir sind windsurfen gegangen	we went windsurfing
wir haben den berühmten Dom besichtigt	we visited the famous cathedral

Expressing likes and dislikes

das Essen hat mir / uns nicht geschmeckt	I / we did not like the food
das Essen war lecker	the food was delicious
die Familie war nett und freundlich	the family was very nice and friendly
das kalte Wetter hat ihm / ihr nicht gefallen	he / she did not like the cold weather
die Party am letzten Abend war super	the party on the last night was great
meine Schule hat er / sie sehr gemocht	he / she really liked my school
schottisches Essen hat ihm / ihr nicht gut geschmeckt	he / she did not like Scottish food
mein Haus hat ihm / ihr gut gefallen	he / she really liked my house
es gab zu viele Touristen am Strand	there were too many tourists on the beach
die Gäste nebenan machten zu viel Lärm	the people in the room next to us made too much noise
das Essen im Hotel war mies / ekelhaft	the food in the hotel was lousy / repulsive

Suggesting whether or not you would repeat the experience

es war eine tolle Erfahrung	it was a great experience
ich bin selbstständiger geworden	I have become more independent
ein Jahr im Ausland würde ich anderen Studenten empfehlen	I would recommend a year abroad to other students
ich möchte nach Köln zurückfahren	I'd like to go back to Cologne
ich möchte lieber nicht nach Koblenz zurückkehren	I would rather not go back to Koblenz
ich würde lieber allein oder mit Freunden fahren	I'd rather go on my own or with friends
ich würde lieber fliegen	I'd prefer to travel by plane
einen Aufenthalt im Ausland würde ich empfehlen	I'd recommend a spell abroad
ich würde nie wieder dahin fahren	I'd never go back there
nächstes Jahr hoffe ich, ihn / sie zu besuchen	I hope to visit him / her next year
mit meiner Familie würde ich nie wieder wegfahren	I'd never go away again with my family
einen Schweizer / eine Schweizerin würde ich gern wieder zu mir nach Hause einladen	I would like to invite a Swiss person to my home again
das nächste Mal	the next time
in Zukunft	in future

Giving a reason for your opinion

die Reise war zu lang	the journey was too long
mit der Familie / den Lehrern / meinen Klassenkameraden habe ich mich nicht gut verstanden	I did not get on well with the family / the teachers / my classmates
auf einer Klassenfahrt sind die Lehrer zu streng	teachers are too strict on a school trip
als Gastgeber/in hat es mir keinen Spaß gemacht	I did not enjoy hosting

das Wetter war mir zu heiß und schwül	the weather was too hot and humid for me
wir hatten nichts gemeinsam	we didn't have anything in common
die Lehrer waren zu streng	the teachers were too strict
ich habe zu viel Geld ausgegeben	I spent too much money
ich wurde von Mücken gestochen	I was bitten by mosquitoes
ich hatte einen Sonnenbrand	I had sunburn
es fiel mir schwer, die Sprache zu verstehen	I had difficulty understanding the language
sie haben zu schnell geredet	they talked too fast
von einem sprachlichen Standpunkt aus	from a linguistic point of view
ich habe meinen Aufenthalt voll ausgenutzt	I made the most of my stay
die Party war eine reine Katastrophe	the party was a complete disaster
meine Eltern behandelten mich wie ein Kind	my parents treated me like a child
schade, dass es nur zwei Wochen waren!	it's a shame it only lasted two weeks!
ich habe eine herrliche Zeit verbracht	I had the time of my life

Describing the job you did

ich habe als Spüler/in gearbeitet Kellner/in Au-pair-Mädchen	I worked as a dishwasher waiter / waitress an au-pair
die Arbeit war einfach / schwer / anstrengend	the work was easy / hard / stressful
ich musste hart arbeiten	I had to work hard
ich habe von acht Uhr morgens bis sechs Uhr abends gearbeitet	I worked from eight in the morning till six in the evening
die Arbeit war schlecht bezahlt	the job was badly paid

manchmal habe ich viel Trinkgeld bekommen	sometimes I got a lot of tips
der Stundenlohn war mies	the hourly rate was lousy
jeden Morgen musste ich früh aufstehen	every morning I had to get up early
jeden Morgen fing ich um neun Uhr an zu arbeiten	every morning I started my work at nine

Describing the weather

das Wetter war wunderschön	the weather was marvellous
jeden Morgen hat es geschneit	it snowed every morning
die meiste Zeit war das Wetter schön	the weather was nice most of the time
abends war es stürmisch	it was stormy in the evening

END OF UNIT READING TESTS

LIFESTYLES

Passage 1

Allein oder im Hotel Mama?

Niemand wartet auf Mathias (20), wenn er von der Schule nach Hause
kommt. „Die Wohnung ist leer. Das Essen steht nicht auf dem Tisch. Ich
lebe allein, seit ich 17 Jahre alt bin", erklärt er. Für den Schüler bedeutet
das: Er kümmert sich um den ganzen Haushalt selbst. Einkaufen, kochen,
5   waschen, putzen. Sein Alltag ist ziemlich stressig. Seine Freunde
verstehen das oft nicht. „Du bist doch jung und lebst nur einmal."

Die Eltern von Mathias haben sich scheiden lassen. Er wohnte zuerst bei
seiner Mutter. Die zog dann aber in eine andere Stadt. „Ich wollte wegen
meiner Freunde bleiben. Außerdem verstand ich mich damals nicht so gut
10 mit ihr", erklärt er. Sein Vater arbeitet im Ausland. Zu ihm hat er kaum
Kontakt. Im letzten Jahr hat Mathias ihn nur zwei Wochen gesehen. „Als er
einmal wieder zu Besuch war, saß ich gerade auf meinen gepackten
Sachen. Ich wusste nicht, wohin", erinnert er sich. Der Vater bot ihm seine
ungenutzte Wohnung im Haus der Großeltern an. Das Angebot gefiel
15 Mathias: „Nach den Streitereien mit meiner Mutter wollte ich frei und
unabhängig sein. Ich wollte mein eigenes Leben führen." Am Anfang
kümmert sich noch die Großmutter um den Jungen. Sie bekochte und
bemutterte ihn. „Das wollte ich nicht, und das habe ich ihr gesagt. Ich
wollte mich damals niemandem verpflichtet fühlen."

20 Mathias lebt gerne allein, auch wenn er oft wenig Zeit hat. Tagsüber isst er
oft nichts. Abends muss es dann schnell gehen. Tiefkühlpizza, Eier und
Spaghetti stehen auf seinem Speiseplan ganz oben. „Ich habe keine Lust,
für mich alleine zu kochen. Das ist mir zu aufwendig und kostet zu viel Zeit",
bekennt er. Haushalt ist für ihn eigentlich nur Nebensache. Hat er keine
25 Zeit, bleibt der Abwasch schon mal liegen. Trotzdem hat er alles gut im Griff.
„Wer kaum zu Hause ist, macht auch keinen Dreck", kommentiert er.

Bei Sascha (20) steht nach der Schule das Mittagessen auf dem Tisch.
Wenn seine Mutter nicht gekocht hat, bedient er sich am Kühlschrank. Er
lebt noch zu Hause bei seinen Eltern. „Das ist doch heute normal", meint er.
30 „Ich kenne viele Jugendliche, die noch bei ihren Eltern wohnen. Die
meisten können es sich nicht leisten auszuziehen."

Besonders im Sommer geht Sascha gern und ausgiebig mit seinen Freunden auf Parties. Manchmal kommt er spät in der Nacht – oder früh morgens! – nach Hause. Dann reden ihm die Eltern schon mal ins
35 Gewissen. Natürlich hat er das nicht so gerne. „Das ist manchmal nervig, aber auch verständlich", findet er. Ansonsten versteht er sich gut mit seinen Eltern. Parties kündigt er aus Rücksicht vorher an.

Für Sascha spielt das Familienleben eine große Rolle. Er weiß: „Egal, was passiert, meine Eltern stehen immer hinter mir. Sie unterstützen mich und
40 geben mir den Rückhalt und die Sicherheit, die ich brauche."

Questions

1. What does Mathias find when he comes home from school? **2 points**

2. Mention two household chores he has to see to himself. **2 points**

3. What do his friends think about his stressful daily routine? **1 point**

4. Why did he not want to live with his mother? **2 points**

5. What offer did his father make? **1 point**

6. Why did this arrangement suit Mathias? **2 points**

7. How did his grandmother treat him at first? **2 points**

8. Apart from spaghetti, mention two meals he will often prepare for himself. **2 points**

9. Why can he not be bothered cooking for himself? **2 points**

10. What is his attitude towards the washing-up? **1 point**

11. What final comment does he make about people who are often out? **1 point**

12. According to Sascha, why do many young people live with their parents? **1 point**

13. What does he often like doing in the summer? **1 point**

14. How do his parents react when he comes home late? **1 point**

15. Why is family life so important to him? **3 points**

24 points

Passage 2

Allein sein

Wie wollt ihr lieber leben – solo oder mit Partner?

Martin ist 16 und Single. In seiner Freizeit spielt er oft Fußball. „Es gibt
einfach Dinge, die man mit Jungen besser machen kann. Zum Beispiel
Fußball spielen! Viele Mädchen verstehen nicht warum Fußball bei so
vielen Jungen so wichtig ist. Wenn mich ein Mädchen von meinen
5   Freunden wegbringen will, werde ich böse", erzält er. Martin fühlt
sich wohl[1] als Single.

Auch Elke, 15 Jahre, Sharon, 14 Jahre, und Simon, 16 Jahre, fühlen sich
gut allein. Elkes letzte Beziehung liegt noch gar nicht so lange zurück. Vor
einer Woche hat sie sich von ihrem Freund getrennt. „Er hat mich einfach
10   nicht so nett behandelt und ständig versetzt", berichtet sie. „Irgendwann ist
einfach Schluss." Auch ihre Freundin Sharon meint, dass man nicht um
jeden Preis eine Beziehung halten sollte. Ihre letzte endete auf einer
Klassenfahrt. Das Datum weiß sie noch ganz genau. Die Freundschaft war
etwas ganz Besonderes für sie. „Aber ich habe mehr gegeben als
15   bekommen", erklärt sie den Grund für die Trennung. Die anderen Mädchen
aus ihrer Clique haben alle einen Freund. Doch das stört Elke und Sharon
nicht. Sie fühlen sich nicht unter Druck gesetzt. Auch wenn Beziehung ein
wichtiges Gesprächsthema ist.

Es kann auch Vorteile haben ein Single zu sein. „Wenn ich auf eine Party
20   gehe, kann ich mich mit vielen Leuten unterhalten. Ich kann auch mal mit
den gut aussehenden Jungs flirten. Meine Freundinnen sitzen immer bei
ihren Freunden und können das nicht", meint Elke. Natürlich kennt sie auch
die Vorteile einer Beziehung: „Man hat jemanden, zu dem man gehen kann,
wenn man Probleme hat. Und der das Gleiche für mich empfindet wie ich
25   für ihn." Doch auf der Suche nach einem neuen Partner ist sie nicht. Darin
ist sie sich mit den anderen einig. Egal, wie lange ihre letzte Beziehung
zurückliegt. Elke, Sharon und Martin haben es nicht eilig, in einer
Beziehung zu sein.

Und Simon? „Es klappt am besten, wenn man es auf sich einfach
30   zukommen lässt", weiß er. Simon war ein Jahr mit einem Mädchen
zusammen. Dann trennte er sich von ihr. Der Grund war ihre Untreue.

Wenn jetzt die „Richtige" kommt, würde er seine Freiheit gegen eine Partnerschaft tauschen. Sofort! „Als Single fühlt man sich oft allein!", hat er erlebt. Andererseits ist ihm wichtig, auch Zeit für sich selbst zu haben.

35 „Manchmal wünscht man sich eine feste Partnerin", gibt Martin zu. „Dann hat man immer jemanden, mit dem man etwas unternehmen kann." Trotzdem findet er, dass Freunde und die Familie wichtiger sind. Simon, Sharon und Elke stimmen ihm zu. „Wenn eine Partnerschaft auseinander geht, ist Schluss und die meisten sehen einen danach nicht mehr. Freunde
40 aber sind immer für einen da", sagt Simon. Später, ab 30, da kann dann eine richtige Beziehung und eine Familie kommen.

Bis dahin wollen alle erst einmal Erfahrungen sammeln. Vielleicht trifft man ja jemanden, mit dem man bis ans Lebensende zusammen ist. „Da ist aber unwahrscheinlich!", meint Martin. Schließlich ist man ja noch nicht
45 einmal 18!

[1] sich wohl fühlen: to feel happy

Questions

1. *(a)* Give two reasons why Martin prefers to be single.   **2 points**

    (b) What makes him angry   **1 point**

2. Why did Elke end her last relationship   **2 points**

3. *(a)* When did Sharon's last relationship end?   **1 point**

    (b) Why did she end it?   **1 point**

4. According to Elke, what advantages are there in

    (a) being single?   **2 points**

    (b) being in a relationship?   **2 points**

5. What do Elke, Sharon and Martin all have in common?   **1 point**

6. *(a)* What caused Simon to end his relationship?   **1 point**

    (b) Why would he exchange his freedom for the 'right' person?   **1 point**

    (c) However, what is important to him?   **1 point**

7. Why would Martin like a steady partner?   **1 point**

8. Why do Simon, Sharon and Elke all consider friends and family more
    important than a partner?   **2 points**

9. What does Simon hope for in his 30s?   **2 points**

10. *(a)* What are Martin and his friends going to do in the meantime?   **2 points**

    (b) What final comment does he make about this?   **1 point**

                                                                                          23 points

Passage 3

Ein ganz normales Leben

„Ich heiße Monika, bin 19 Jahre alt, lebe in Kiel in einer 3-Zimmer-Wohnung, habe einen Hund und eine Katze, bin allein stehend und im Moment arbeitslos. Ansonsten gibt es noch zu erklären, dass ich im Rollstuhl lebe.

5   Das größte Problem als Behinderte sind für mich die öffentlichen Toiletten. Die sind nicht breit genug, und das Personal ist nicht in der Lage, einem zu helfen … Und in Warenhäusern sind die Fahrstühle oftmals auch zu klein. Und dann, wenn ich über die Straße will, gibt es immer noch viele Bürgersteige, die zu hoch sind." Das sind nur einige von vielen
10   praktischen Problemen, die Monika hat, wenn sie in Kiel unterwegs ist.

Sie hat vor drei Jahren einen Unfall gehabt, der ihr Leben veränderte: „Ich wollte morgens zur Schule. Ich habe damals in einem Vorort von Kiel gewohnt und musste mit dem Zug in die Stadt fahren. Am Bahnhof ist der Zug gerade losgefahren, und ich habe versucht, die Tür aufzureißen, damit
15   ich noch mitfahren konnte. Als die Tür aufgesprungen ist, bin ich gestolpert und unter den Zug gefallen … Wenn die Leute fragen, warum ich keine Beine habe, und ich erzähle, dass ich beim Aufspringen unter den Zug gekommen bin, dann denken die meisten, ich wollte vor den Zug springen, mich also umbringen. Deshalb sage ich eben, ich hatte einen Autounfall,
20   und dann ist das Thema für mich erledigt."

Heute versucht Monika, ein ganz normales Leben zu führen. Sie versucht, alles zu machen, was ihre gleichaltrigen Freunde und Freundinnen auch tun. „Ich würde gerne mal mit meinem Hund allein in den Wald gehen. Das ist nicht möglich, weil der Wald ja Natur ist und die Wege dort nicht
25   gepflastert sind. Auch am Strand muss ich immer jemand dabei haben, wegen dem Sand." Trotzdem möchte sie unabhängig sein. Daher lebt sie auch mit Hund und Katze in einer eigenen kleinen Wohnung und macht den ganzen Haushalt alleine. Sie ist außerdem sehr unternehmungslustig[1] und viel mit ihrem neuen Auto unterwegs.

30   „Auto??" – „Ja, den Führerschein habe ich gemacht, als ich in Hamburg im Krankenhaus war. Da gibt es eine Fahrschule, die ein Behindertenfahrzeug hat. Da lernt man ganz normal Auto fahren wie jeder andere auch. Das ist

auch so ein Punkt. Immer wieder erlebe ich, dass die Behindertenparkplätze von Nichtbehinderten besetzt sind."

35 Was sie nur schwer verkraften[2] kann, sind die Vorurteile der Menschen. „Die Leute sehen mich nicht als Person, sondern als Behinderte, und eine Behinderte ist ja in unserer Gesellschaft keine Person und hat vor allem keine Persönlichkeit. Diese Meinung finde ich irgendwie traurig heutzutage."

[1] unternehmungslustig: adventurous
[2] verkraften: to cope with

Questions

1. What is Monika's current marital and professional status? **2 points**

2. What problems does she face
   (a) in public toilets. **2 points**
   (b) in department stores? **1 point**
   (c) when she wants to cross the street? **1 point**

3. *(a)* Describe the accident at the station which changed her life forever. **3 points**
   (b) What do most people think when she tells them of her accident? **1 point**
   (c) What lie does she end up telling them? **1 point**

4. *(a)* Mention two things Monika would like to do on her own in her wheelchair and why this is not possible. **4 points**
   (b) Mention two things she does on her own which show her independence. **2 points**

5. *(a)* Give details of how she learned to drive. **3 points**
   (b) As a disabled driver, what problems does she face again and again? **1 point**

6. What prejudice in society does Monika find hard to cope with? **2 points**

23 points

Passage 4

Kein Appetit auf Fleisch

Sarah und Laura (14) sind seit ihrem elften Lebensjahr Vegetarier. Früher kam in ihrer Familie fast täglich Fleisch auf den Tisch. Heute essen die Zwillinge lieber Pizza Margarita anstatt Spaghetti Bolognese. Mittags, wenn Sarah und Laura von der Schule kommen, wird zu Hause nur noch
5 vegetarisch gekocht. „Warum wir kein Fleisch mögen? Das fragen uns viele. Wir ekeln uns einfach nur davor." Sprüche wie „Fleisch ist doch das Leckerste, was es gibt" müssen sie sich immer wieder anhören. Doch das sehen die beiden anders: „Nahrung ist etwas sehr Natürliches. Doch bei Fleisch ist nicht mehr viel davon übrig." Das wissen sogar viele Nicht-
10 Vegetarier. Rinderwahnsinn, Massentierhaltung und Tiertransportskandale haben vielen den Appetit verdorben[1].

Astrid Viell (49) unterrichtet Sarah und Laura in Biologie. Sie spricht ein anderes Problem an: „Viele Tiere werden mit Antibiotika gefüttert[2]. Der Mensch nimmt das mit dem Fleisch auf. Dadurch werden Antibiotika bei
15 Menschen immer unwirksamer." An ihrer Schule gibt es ungefähr einen Vegetarier pro Klasse. Hauptsächlich sind es Mädchen, die sich fleischlos ernähren. „Viele sagen, dass sie Tiere lieb haben. Das Schlachten finden sie grausam", sagt die Lehrerin.

Durch das Töten eines Tieres sind auch Ümmihan (15) und Ines (11) zu
20 überzeugten Vegetarierinnen geworden. Bei Ümmihan war es das rituelle Schlachten am moslemischen Opferfest, das sie vor acht Jahren erlebte. Seitdem verzichtet[3] sie wie ihre vier älteren Schwestern auf Fleisch. Ines machte Reitferien auf einem Bauernhof, als sie dort ein geschlachtetes Rind hängen sah. „Darunter konnte man noch die Blutlachen sehen",
25 erinnert sie sich angeekelt[4]. In diesem Augenblick wurde ihr bewusst, was sie eigentlich aß. Ihre ältere Schwester Denise (14), wie Ines eine leidenschaftliche Reiterin, isst ebenfalls kein Fleisch. Beide sind überzeugt, damit den Tieren helfen zu können: „Wenn es viele Menschen machen, schadet das der Fleischindustrie."

30 Auch wenn sich viele über das Töten von Tieren aufregen, die Konsequenzen ziehen[5] nur wenige. So sehen es jedenfalls Jennifer (12) und Jenny (12): „Die meisten Teenager machen sich keine Gedanken, wenn sie mal wieder zum Hamburger greifen." Ihren eigenen Fleischverzicht sehen sie auch als Anstoß[6] für andere. „Es ist gut zu
35 wissen, dass man es tut", meint Jennifer.

Für Yasmin (14) war es zunächst eine reine Mitmach-Aktion. Ihre Freundin verzichtete aus gesundheitlichen Gründen auf Fleisch. Yasmin wollte sehen, ob sie es auch schafft. „Durch den Eiweißentzug[7] bekam ich Kreislaufprobleme. Zum Ausgleich aß ich mehr Fisch und Sojafleisch."
40 Heute glaubt sie, dass sie sich gesünder als früher ernährt. Anstatt Süßigkeiten isst sie mehr Obst und Gemüse. Gewichtsprobleme kennt sie nicht.

Lisa (11) wäre am liebsten Veganerin. Doch ihre Mutter sorgte sich um ihre Gesundheit. Deshalb versprach sie, einmal in der Woche Eier und Fisch zu
45 essen. Legebatterien mit eingepferchten[8] Hühnern lehnt Lisa ab. Darum kauft ihre Mutter jetzt nur noch Eier aus Bodenhaltung beim Bauern. Zu Hause kümmert sie sich liebevoll um ihre Haustiere. Und die will man ja auch nicht schlachten und essen!

[1] verderben: to spoil
[2] füttern: to feed
[3] verzichten: to do without / to give up
[4] angeekelt: disgusted
[5] die Konsequenzen ziehen: to take the logical step
[6] der Anstoß: impetus
[7] der Eiweißentzug: lack of protein
[8] eingepfercht: penned in / caged

Questions

1. How long have Sarah and Laura been vegetarian? **1 point**

2. Why was this such a dramatic change for them? **1 point**

3. What reason do they give for not liking meat? **1 point**

4. Mention three negative aspects of the meat trade which might spoil your appetite. **3 points**

5. What problematic food chain does the biology teacher mention? **3 points**

6. What statistic are we given regarding the number of vegetarians at her school? **1 point**

7. What reason is given for the high number of female vegetarians? **2 points**

8. What in particular prompted
   (a) Ümmihan **1 point**
   (b) and Ines to give up eating meat? **2 points**

9. What effect do Ines and Denise think their vegetarianism will have on
   (a) animals? **1 point**
   (b) the meat industry? **1 point**

10. What point do Jennifer and Jenny make about most teenagers? **1 point**

11. Why did Yasmin give up meat? **2 points**

12. What did she have to do to compensate for the lack of protein in her new diet? **1 point**

13. What benefit has she noticed with her new, healthy diet? **1 point**

14. What does Lisa's mother have to buy for her daughter? **1 point**

15. What final comment is made about domestic animals? **1 point**

24 points

EDUCATION AND WORK

Passage 5

Ein Ehrenamt[1]

Sie machen einen Job, aber bekommen kein Geld dafür. Trotzdem haben
Semir, Anne und die anderen jede Menge Spaß. Sie finden, dass ein
Ehrenamt[1] eine gute Sache ist, weil man Verantwortung übernimmt und
Vertrauen erhält.

5   „Seit drei Jahren trainiere ich die jüngsten Kicker des Fußballvereins,
zusammen mit einem Co-Trainer Christian," erzählt Semir (18). „Ein
Kollege hatte mir diesen Job angeboten. Ich dachte: ich versuche es mal.
Mir macht es rießig viel Spaß. Wir haben zwei Gruppen mit 34 Spielern.
Die Begeisterung der Jungs ist toll. Die haben nie schlechte Laune. Ich
10 selbst spiele in einem anderen Verein Fußball. Trotzdem will ich hier
Trainer bleiben. Ich profitiere von dem Kicken mit den Kleinen. Früher bin
ich nur wie blöd gerannt. Jetzt weiß ich, dass man auch Dehnungsübungen,
Lauf- und Gymnastiktraining braucht. Ganz wichtig: Wir versuchen den
Jungs ‚Fairplay' beizubringen. Unser Motto ist ‚Sich immer vertragen!'"

15 Anne singt wahnsinnig gern. „Beim gemeinsamen Üben geht es mir immer
gut. Seit über sieben Jahren singe ich im Chor des Ruhrgymnasiums.
Irgendwann hat mich der Chorleiter angesprochen. Ich sollte mithelfen.
Seitdem leite ich manchmal unsere Proben. Außerdem mache ich
Werbeplakate für unsere Aufführungen. Ich gestalte sie am Computer.
20 Dann gehe ich in Geschäfte. Ich bitte darum, dass man die Plakate
aushängt. Insgesamt geht viel Zeit dafür drauf – auch das Wochenende.
Doch man lernt eine Menge. Wir singen klassische und moderne Musik: die
Carmina Burana von Carl Orff oder Stücke der Beatles. Letzte Weihnachten
haben wir *City of Light* gesungen, ein Singspiel aus Amerika. Das Beste ist
25 aber die Gemeinschaft unter uns 50 Leuten."

Arne ist 17 und ist in seiner evangelischen Kirchengemeinde aktiv. „Seit
zwei Jahren helfe ich bei Jugendfreizeiten. Im August fahre ich mit 13- bis
17-jährigen Schülern nach Frankreich. Meine Freunde und ich bereiten die
Fahrten an mehreren Abenden vor. Wir entwerfen das Programm mit
30 Konzerten, Spielen und Gottesdiensten. Wir kümmern uns um die
Unterkunft, die Verpflegung, die Reiseapotheke, die Zimmerverteilung und
den Spüldienst. Bei der Planung gibt es meistens viel zu lachen. Während

der Reise ist man für vieles verantwortlich. Man muss auf vieles achten. Schön ist, dass man viele Leute und verschiedene Landschaften kennen
35 lernt. Selbst, wenn man vorher viel Arbeit hatte."

Sabrina (17) und Anna (18) betreuen die Mädchenturngruppe ihres Turnvereins. „Das machen wir seit fast drei Jahren. Unsere ‚Babys' sind 6 bis 11 Jahre alt. 15 bis 20 Mädels kommen regelmäßig. Am schönsten finden sie das Turnen auf Bodenmatten. Auch für uns sind die
40 Übungsstunden ein gutes Training. Wir genießen unsere Zeit mit den Kleinen, weil sie viel weniger Sorgen haben als wir, und wenn sie uns Geschichten aus ihrem Alltag erzählen, vergessen wir unsere eigenen Probleme. Kurz gesagt, haben sie Vertrauen zu uns. Das ist die Belohnung für unsere Zeit und Mühe. Wir möchten dieses Ehrenamt noch lange
45 machen."

[1] ein Ehrenamt: voluntary work

Questions

1. Why do Semir, Anne and the others think voluntary work is a good thing?   **2 points**

2. What exactly is Semir's job?   **1 point**

3. What does he particularly like about working with the boys?   **2 points**

4. How have his own skills improved in working with the boys?   **3 points**

5. What is their motto?   **1 point**

6. *(a)* Which hobby did Anne start over seven years ago?   **1 point**

   (b) Mention two tasks she now carries out.   **2 points**

7. What is Arne doing in August?   **1 point**

8. Mention two activities he and his friends are planning.   **2 points**

9. Mention three things they have to see to.   **3 points**

10. What does he find enjoyable on the trip itself?   **1 point**

11. What sort of work do Sabrina and Anna do?   **2 points**

12. Why do the trainers enjoy their time with the girls?   **3 points**

    24 points

Passage 6

Traumberuf Schauspieler?

Ein Casting

Hinter einem Schreibtisch sitzen zwei Frauen und ein Mann: die Produzentin, die Produktions-Managerin und der Regisseur. Sie unterhalten sich über die Schauspieler, deren Lebensläufe und Fotos vor ihnen auf einem Stapel liegen. Sie werden heute mit zwanzig
5 Schauspielern sprechen, die für die beiden Hauptrollen in einer Fernsehserie gekommen sind. Und hoffentlich werden sie die richtigen Schauspieler finden, die Nils und Sandra spielen können, die in einer Wohngemeinschaft wohnen und jede Menge Probleme mit ihren Nachbarn haben.

10 Die ersten Schauspieler kommen ins Zimmer. Sie setzen sich und man unterhält sich kurz darüber, wie sich die Produzentin und der Regisseur die beiden Charaktere vorstellen. Dann geht es los. Die Schauspieler spielen die erste Szene. Nachdem sie fertig sind, spricht der Regisseur wieder mit ihnen. Er lobt sie und erklärt ihnen, wie sie ihre Rolle noch besser gestalten
15 können. Dann wird dieselbe Szene noch einmal gespielt und gleichzeitig gefilmt, damit sich der Regisseur und der Programm-Chef die Schauspieler auch später wieder ansehen können. Nach dem Ende der Szene gibt es wieder ein kurzes Lob. Die Produzentin schlägt vor, die beiden auch ein Stück Text für zwei Nebenrollen sprechen zu lassen. Die Schauspieler
20 bekommen ihre Texte und ziehen sich in einen Nebenraum zurück, um sich den Text in Ruhe anzusehen.

Als die Schauspieler im Nebenraum sind, unterhalten sich die Produzentin und der Regisseur: „Was hältst du von ihm?" „Er ist ein sehr guter Schauspieler, sehr gut, aber ich hatte mir Nils größer vorgestellt – und
25 sportlicher. Ich weiß nicht, ob er der richtige Typ ist." „Mmmh, ja da hast du Recht. Aber sie ist gut, findest du nicht?" „Ja, sie spielt Sandra sehr gut. Sie hat genau verstanden, was wir wollen. Aber ihre Haare. Die sehen schrecklich aus. Glaubst du, wir können da etwas machen?" „Ja, das ist kein Problem."

30 Die Schauspieler kommen zurück und zeigen noch einmal, was sie können. Danach werden sie mit den Worten: „Falls wir Sie für eine Rolle auswählen,

melden wir uns nächste Woche bei Ihnen." verabschiedet. Danach kommen
die nächsten beiden . . .

Eine Woche später

35 Die junge Schauspielerin bereitet sich gerade auf ein neues Casting vor, als
das Telefon klingelt. Es ist ihre Agentin. Sie gratuliert ihr und freut sich,
dass sie die Rolle der Sandra in der neuen Fernsehserie bekommen hat.
Es ist ihre erste große Rolle nach etwa 50 Castings und einer kleinen
Nebenrolle in einem Krimi, in dem sie eine Putzfrau spielte.

40 Als das Telefon des Schauspielers klingelt, ist er nicht zu Hause. Er arbeitet
gerade als Kellner in einem Restaurant. Nach seiner Arbeit trifft er sich dann
mit Freunden, mit denen er ein Theaterstück für Kinder einstudiert. Das
wollen sie im Sommer im Park aufführen. Um Mitternacht kommt er nach
Hause und hört seinen Anrufbeantworter ab. Er hört die Nachricht, dass er
die Rolle des Nils nicht bekommen hat. „Macht nichts", sagt er zu sich
45 selbst. „Das nächste Casting kommt bestimmt. Man muss einfach
dranbleiben."

Questions

1. Who are the three people on the selection panel? **3 points**

2. What do they have on a pile in front of them? **2 points**

3. What are we told about the two characters? **2 points**

4. What is the first thing that is discussed with the actors? **1 point**

5. What response do the actors get after their attempt at the first scene? **2 points**

6. After the filming what are they asked to do? **1 point**

7. Once the casting team is alone again what comments are made about the actor hoping to play Nils? **1 point**

8. Why do they think he is not right for the part? **2 points**

9. What do they not like about the actress? **1 point**

10. What is the actress doing when her phone call comes? **1 point**

11. *(a)* Why has this latest audition been particularly successful for her? **2 points**

    (b) What other acting experience has she had? **2 points**

12. *(a)* Why is the actor not at home when he is called? **1 point**

    (b) What is he doing later with friends? **1 point**

13. How does he respond to the message on his answering machine? **2 points**

24 points

THE WIDER WORLD

Passage 7

Im Rhythmus des Orients

Es ist Samstagabend, 23 Uhr – für Diskobesucher also noch früh am Abend. Doch im *Bodrum* ist die Tanzfläche schon voll. Gut gekleidete Jugendliche tanzen begeistert zu der Musik, die aus den Lautsprechern schallt. Diskjockey Ufak kennt sein Publikum: Orientalische Klänge sind gefragt. Nur

5 ganz selten hört man einmal einen englischen Titel. Der Name der Disko, das Publikum, die Musik: Man denkt, man sei in der Türkei. Doch das *Bodrum* ist Deutschlands größte türkische Disko. Sie liegt mitten in Köln unter einem Einkaufszentrum. Auf 700 Quadratmetern Kellerraum gibt es eine große und mehrere kleine Tanzflächen. Buntes Licht zuckt[1] im

10 Rhythmus der Musik.

Vor wenigen Monaten war hier noch ein schlecht besuchtes Lokal. Einige Theken erinnern noch an die altdeutsche Einrichtung. Die neuen Besitzer wollten kein Risiko eingehen: sie investierten nur das Nötigste. Denn zunächst war das *Bodrum* ein Test-Projekt. Keiner wusste, ob die Idee

15 ankam. Hussein Furol leitet das Bodrum mit zwei Freunden. „Den türkischen Jugendlichen fehlte in deutschen Diskos oft etwas. Sie kannten die türkische Musik aus ihren Ferien in der Türkei und vermissten sie hier in Deutschland. Mit dem *Bodrum* wollte ich ihnen einen Ort geben, wo sie ihre Musik hören und dazu tanzen könnten."

20 Der Erfolg gibt ihm recht. Jeden Freitag und Samstag sind die Tanzflächen voll. „Wegen der Musik ist das *Bodrum* ein Stück Türkei, ein Stück Heimat für mich", sagt Kemal, ein junger Deutsch-Türke*. Jashdan und Ipek erzählen: „Wir kommen sehr oft her. Wir kennen sehr viele Leute hier. Das *Bodrum* ist für uns so eine Art Jugendzentrum, wo sich alle Jugendlichen

25 gerne treffen. Das liegt an der tollen Atmosphäre. Stimmung kann man überall schaffen, aber diese Atmosphäre nicht. Wir fühlen uns sehr wohl!"

Es gibt aber noch einen Grund, warum viele türkische Jugendliche ins *Bodrum* kommen. Darüber berichten Ömer und Baçar: „Wir hatten Probleme, in deutsche Diskos hineinzukommen. Die Türsteher sagten uns:

30 ‚Ihr seid zu schlecht angezogen, ich kann euch nicht hineinlassen.' Wir sahen aber genauso aus wie alle anderen auch. In Wirklichkeit wollten sie keine Ausländer in der Disko haben. So etwas kann uns hier nicht passieren!"

Berrun erzählt, was ihre deutschen Freundinnen in anderen Kölner Diskos
35 nicht erleben: „Einige traditionellere türkische Mädchen hier dürfen nur mit
einem Bruder oder Cousin als Begleiter kommen und nicht mit fremden
jungen Männern tanzen." Darum sieht man viele Mädchengruppen auf der
Tanzfläche. Andererseits gibt es auch viele tanzende und flirtende Paare.
Größere Probleme zwischen „traditionell" und „modern" denkenden
40 Jugendlichen gab es jedoch noch nicht.

Furol und sein Bodrum-Team wollen darum noch einen Schritt weitergehen.
Man will die Diskothek ausbauen und ein türkisches Restaurant eröffnen.
Furol hofft, dass dann mehr deutsche Jugendliche kommen: Vielleicht
vermischen sich die zwei Kulturen ja eines Tages im Nachtleben …

*Deutsch-Türken nennen sich die türkischen Jugendlichen, die in Deutschland
aufgewachsen sind, weil schon ihre Eltern nach Deutschland gekommen sind.

[1] zucken: to flash

Questions

1. (a) Why is it surprising to find the *Bodrum* dance floor full at 11 pm?   **1 point**

    (b) What is the most requested sort of music?   **1 point**

    (c) Where exactly is the disco situated?   **2 points**

2. (a) What existed on the site until a few months ago?   **1 point**

    (b) Why do some of the original furnishings still exist?   **3 points**

3. (a) According to Hussein Furol, what were young Turks missing in German discos?   **1 point**

    (b) What was his intention in opening the *Bodrum*?   **1 point**

4. (a) Why does Kemal like coming to the *Bodrum*?   **1 point**

    (b) Why do Jashdan and Ipek often come to the *Bodrum*?   **3 points**

5. (a) What happened to Ömer and Baçar at German discos?   **2 points**

    (b) What evidence was there that this was racially motivated?   **1 point**

6. What are we told about some of the more traditional Turkish girls in the disco?   **2 points**

7. (a) What plans are afoot for the *Bodrum*?   **2 points**

    (b) What is Furol's wish for the future?   **2 points**

    23 points

Passage 8

In England herrscht nicht nur Nebel

Julius, ein 18-jähriger Schüler aus Bonn, wollte ein Jahr in England
verbringen. Er landete in einem Internat in Reading, 60km westlich von
London. „Während meine deutschen Klassenkameraden Bodenturnen
machen mussten, spielte ich Rugby," sagt der begeisterte Fußballspieler
5 heute.

Anfangs empfand er die Umstellung[1] von einer deutschen Gesamtschule zu
einem englischen Internat als sehr groß. „Der Tagesablauf ist dort einfach
sehr viel strukturierter," resümiert Julius und lächelt. „Im Vergleich zu
Deutschland muß man sich erst einmal daran gewöhnen, jeden Tag erst um
10 8 Uhr aufzustehen und länger im Bett zu bleiben!"

Der normale Schultag lief folgendermaßen[2] ab: Nach dem Treffen der
gesamten Schule in der Aula um halb neun begann die erste Stunde. Bis
zum Mittagessen um 13 Uhr standen 5 Stunden auf dem Plan. Das
Mittagessen bestand meistens aus britischem Rindfleisch, Kartoffeln und
15 Gemüse. „Es hat eigentlich ganz gut geschmeckt." Bis um 4 Uhr musste
man sich nun sportlich betätigen. Je nach Trimester spielte man die typisch
britischen Sportarten Rugby, Fußball oder Kricket. Ein Kricketspiel dauert 5
Tage. „Super in Zeiten vieler Arbeiten, weil man sich beim Spielen
entspannen kann. Aber es macht überhaupt keinen Spaß, wenn es regnet!"
20 Nach den letzten beiden Unterrichtsstunden am späten Nachmittag und nach
dem Abendessen hatte man eine Stunde Zeit für Hobbys. Zwischen 19 und
21 Uhr wurden auf den Zimmern Hausaufgaben gemacht. „Danach gings
ab in die Kneipe!" Dies widersprach zwar den Regeln der Schule, doch alle,
denen Alkohol verkauft werden konnte, kümmerten sich nicht darum. „Es
25 blieb jedoch wenig Zeit besoffen zu werden, da um zehn Uhr die Häuser
abgeschlossen wurden ... und wenn jemand mit einer Fahne[3] erwischt
wurde, konnte er seine Sachen für die Heimreise schon packen."

Julius war nicht allein im großen England. Ein Drittel der Schüler des
Internats stammte nicht aus dem Vereinigten Königreich. Erfreut berichtet
30 er: „Ich habe jetzt Freunde in Brunei, Südkorea, Brasilien und Hongkong!"

Die ersten drei Monate in dieser fremden Umgebung fielen ihm recht
schwer, doch als er in einer Theatergruppe und als Kapitän der
Fußballmannschaft einige Freunde gewonnen hatte, bereitete ihm das

Leben in England so viel Vergnügen, dass er sich entschied, ein zweites
35 Jahr zu bleiben und auf diese Weise das Abitur in England zu machen.

Jetzt hat er diese Schule verlassen, aber ist immer noch nicht nach
Deutschland zurückgekehrt. Er studiert nun Volkswirtschaft in London. Was
hält er heute von seiner Schulzeit im Internat? „Es waren die besten zwei
Jahre meines Lebens, auch wenn es viele Vorurteile gegen Deutsche in
40 England gibt und die englische Oberstufe[4] sehr hart ist."

PS: Das Wetter ist gar nicht so schlimm wie man immer denkt.

[1] die Umstellung: adjustment
[2] folgendermaßen: in the following way
[3] eine Fahne haben: to reek of alcohol
[4] die Oberstufe: upper school

Questions

1. What sort of school did Julius end up in?   **1 point**

2. How does he contrast his activities with his classmates' in Germany?   **2 points**

3. *(a)* What comment does he make about the daily routine as a boarder?   **1 point**

   (b) Unlike in Germany, what does he have to get used to in England?   **2 points**

4. What happened before the first period?   **1 point**

5. What comment does he make about school lunch?   **1 point**

6. Mention three things he says about cricket.   **3 points**

7. What happened between 7 and 9 pm?   **1 point**

8. In what way did the boarders break the school rules?   **1 point**

9. Why were they unlikely to get drunk?   **2 points**

10. What was the punishment if caught?   **1 point**

11. What information are we given about one third of the boarders?   **1 point**

12. Where did Julius make many of his friends?   **2 points**

13. What decision did he make?   **2 points**

14. What is Julius doing now?   **1 point**

15. What comment does he make about the attitude of the English towards the Germans?   **1 point**

16. What does he say about the English weather?   **1 point**

24 points

Passage 9

Tokyo am Rhein

More than 5500 Japanese work in Düsseldorf. Mai and Yuuki, two Japanese teenagers, live here with their parents.

Mai, 17, und Yuuki, 18, sind in Japan geboren und aufgewachsen. Ihre Väter kamen vor einigen Jahren nach Deutschland und die Familien folgten. „Tokyo am Rhein" – so nennt man Düsseldorf auch. Japanische Geschäfte und Restaurants, aber auch einen Tempel und einen japanischen Garten
5   kann man hier finden. Ein Hauch[1] von Fernost, und das mitten in Deutschland!

Wie erlebten Yuuki und Mai ihren Umzug nach Europa? Yuuki hat sich sehr darüber gefreut. In Japan stand er kurz vor einer wichtigen und schwierigen Prüfung an seiner Schule. „Der Leistungsdruck an einer japanischen
10   Schule ist viel größer als hier", berichtet er. Mai bestätigt das. Heute besuchen beide die „International School of Düsseldorf". Die Unterrichtssprache ist Englisch. Außerdem lernt man Deutsch und Japanisch in einer rein japanischen Klasse.

In der Kantine der Schule gibt es deutsches Essen. Daran haben sich beide
15   erst einmal gewöhnen müssen. Zu Hause kommen japanische Gerichte, viel Reis, Gemüse und Fleisch auf den Tisch; traditionell essen beide Familien mit Stäbchen. Ansonsten ist ihr Lebensstil aber sehr westlich orientiert, sagt Mais Vater in fließendem Deutsch. Von ihm hat Mai sehr viel über Deutschland erfahren – er hat das Land schon als Student bereist und
20   kennen gelernt. Mai schätzt vor allem die Natur an Deutschland. „Hier kann man sehr gut spazieren gehen. In der Nähe unseres Wohnhauses gibt es einen Wald", erzählt sie. Ganz anders dagegen sei es in Japan! „Die Familien machen dort selten Spaziergänge in der Natur", meint sie. Anders als in Deutschland sind die Geschäfte in Japan rund um die Uhr geöffnet.
25   Viele Japaner nutzen das Wochenende, um einkaufen zu gehen.

Yuuki hat ein neues Hobby in Deutschland gefunden. Er spielt in seiner Freizeit besonders gern Billard. „In Japan ist das Spiel nicht so stark verbreitet", erklärt er. Die meisten Jugendlichen finden dort Computerspiele viel spannender. Am Wochenende mache ich gern Kendo – zusammen mit
30   deutschen Jugendlichen in einem Sportclub." Wer ihn zu Hause besucht, lernt vor dem Betreten der Wohnung eine japanische Sitte kennen: An der

Wohnungstür bittet der Gastgeber, dass man die Straßenschuhe auszieht.
In seinem Zimmer sitzt Yuuki oft an seinem Computer. Über das Internet hält
er Kontakt mit seinen japanischen Freunden in der Heimat. Im Internet hat
35 er auch eine Homepage eingerichtet. Auf diesen Seiten kann man sich auf
Japanisch oder Englisch über Deutschland informieren. Beispielsweise
über die unübersichtlichen Tarife in den Düsseldorfer Straßen- und U-
Bahnen, wie es sie in Japan nicht gibt.

In zwei Jahren endet der Deutschlandaufenthalt der Väter. Die beiden
40 jungen Japaner haben dann ihren Schulabschluss in der Tasche. Es ist
also möglich, dass sie andere Wege gehen als ihre Eltern. Was sie heute
dazu meinen? Mai freut sich schon darauf, wieder nach Japan zu kommen.
Yuuki dagegen kann sich sehr gut vorstellen, irgendwo anders zu studieren
und zu leben.

[1] ein Hauch: a touch

Questions

1. Mention three things you might be surprised to find in the middle of Düsseldorf. **2 points**

2. *(a)* Why was Yuuki delighted to move to Germany? **1 point**

   (b) What does he say about Japanese schools? **1 point**

   (c) What are the lessons like in his school in Düsseldorf? **2 points**

3. What is the difference between school meals and mealtimes at home? **3 points**

4. *(a)* What does Mai particularly value in Germany? **1 point**

   (b) What does she say about families in Japan? **1 point**

   (c) What information are we given about shopping in Japan? **2 points**

5. What is Yuuki's new hobby? **1 point**

6. What would Japanese young people much rather do? **1 point**

7. Which Japanese custom is carried out at Yuuki's house? **2 points**

8. What can his homepage be used for? **2 points**

9. What will happen in two years? **1 point**

10. What will the two young people have achieved by then? **1 point**

11. What are their plans for the future at the moment? **2 points**

23 points

ANSWER SCHEMES

Passage 1

Allein oder im Hotel Mama?

1. What does Mathias find when he comes home from school?   **2 points**
    - the flat is empty / no one is waiting for him
    - his meal is not on the table

2. Mention two household chores he has to see to himself.   **2 points**
    - shopping
    - cooking
    - washing
    - cleaning
      (any 2)

3. What do his friends think about his stressful daily routine?   **1 point**
    - they often do not understand it
    OR
    - they tell him he is young and only lives once

4. Why did he not want to live with his mother?   **2 points**
    - she moved to another town but he wanted to stay with his friends
    - he was not getting on well with her at that time

5. What offer did his father make?   **1 point**
    - he offered him his vacant flat in Mathias's grandparents' house

6. Why did this arrangement suit Mathias?   **2 points**
    - after the quarrels with his mother he wanted to be free and independent
    - he wanted to lead his own life

7. How did his grandmother treat him at first?   **2 points**
    - she looked after him
    - she cooked for him
    - she mothered him
      (any 2)

8. Apart from spaghetti, mention two meals he will often prepare for himself.   **2 points**
    - frozen pizza
    - eggs

9. Why can he not be bothered cooking for himself?   **2 points**
    - it is costly
    - it takes up too much time / it is time-consuming

10. What is his attitude towards the washing-up?   **1 point**
    - if he does not have enough time he will leave the dishes

11. What final comment does he make about people who are often out?   **1 point**
    - they do not make a mess / they do not make anything dirty

12. According to Sascha, why do many young people live with their parents?   **1 point**
    - most of them cannot afford to move out

13. What does he often like doing in the summer?   **1 point**
    - going to parties with his friends

14. How do his parents react when he comes home late?   **1 point**
    - they have a serious talk with him

15. Why is family life so important to him?   **3 points**
    - whatever happens he knows his parents will stand by him
    - they support him
    - they give him the backing and the security he needs

24 points

(Unit award 15 / 24)

Passage 2

Allein sein

1. *(a)* Give two resons why Martin prefers to be single.   **2 points**
   - some things, such as playing football, can be done better with boys
   - many girls do not understand the importance of football for so many boys

   (b) What makes him angry?   **1 point**
   - when a girl tries to take him away from his friends

2. Why did Elke end her last relationship?   **2 points**
   - her boyfriend did not treat her well
   - he constantly stood her up

3. *(a)* When did Sharon's last relationship end?   **1 point**
   - on a school trip

   (b) Why did she end it?   **1 point**
   - she gave more than she got

4. According to Elke, what advantages are there in

   (a) being single?   **2 points**
   - when she goes to a party she can talk to lots of people
   - and she can flirt with the good-looking boys
   - her female friends sit with their boyfriends and cannot do that (any 2)

   (b) being in a relationship?   **2 points**
   - you have someone to turn to when you have problems
   - feelings can be reciprocated / you can feel the same for each other

5. What do Elke, Sharon and Martin all have in common?   **1 points**
   - they are not in a hurry to be in a relationship

6. *(a)* What caused Simon to end his relationship?   **1 point**
   - his girlfriend was unfaithful / her unfaithfulness

   (b) Why would he exchange his freedom for the 'right' person?   **1 point**
   - being single, he often feels alone / lonely

(c) However, what is important to him? **1 point**
  - to have time to himself

7. Why would Martin like a steady partner? **1 point**
  - there is always someone to do things with

8. Why do Simon, Sharon and Elke all consider friends and family more important than a partner? **2 points**
  - when a relationship falls apart it is over and most people do not see that person again
  - friends are always there for you

9. What does Simon hope for in his 30s? **2 points**
  - a proper relationship
  - a family

10. *(a)* What are Martin and his friends going to do in the meantime? **2 points**
  - gain experience
  - perhaps meet a lifelong partner

  (b) What final comment does he make about this? **1 point**
  - it is unlikely

23 points

(Unit award 14 / 23)

Passage 3

Ein ganz normales Leben

1. What is Monika's current marital and professional status?   **2 points**
    - single
    - unemployed

2. What problems does she face

    (a) in public toilets?   **2 points**
    - they are not wide enough (for the wheelchair)
    - the staff there are not in a position to help

    (b) in department stores?   **1 point**
    - the lifts are often too small

    (c) when she wants to cross the street?   **1 point**
    - there are still many pavements which are too high

3. *(a)* Describe the accident at the station which changed her life forever.   **3 points**
    - the train was just leaving
    - she tried to open the door
    - the door sprang open, she tripped and fell under the train

    (b) What do most people think when she tells them of her accident?   **1 point**
    - she jumped intentionally in front of the train (she wanted to commit suicide)

    (c) What lie doe she end up telling them?   **1 point**
    - she had a car accident

4. *(a)* Mention two things Monika would like to do on her own in her wheelchair and why
           this is not possible.   **4 points**
    - go to woods (the forest) with her dog
    - there are no paved pathways
    - go to the beach
    - she needs someone to be with her because of the sand

    (b) Mention two things she does on her own which show her independence.   **2 points**
    - she lives in her own flat with a cat and a dog
    - she does all the housework on her own
    - she drives about a lot in her new car
      (any 2)

5. (a) Give details of how she learned to drive.   **3 points**
        • when she was in hospital in Hamburg
        • she went to a driving school
        • which had a vehicle for disabled individuals

    (b) As a disabled driver, what problems does she face again and again?   **1 points**
        • parking spaces reserved for disabled people are often taken by
          able-bodied persons

6. What prejudice in society does Monika find hard to cope with?   **2 points**
        • she is not seen as an individual but as a disabled person
        • a disabled person in our society is seen to have no personality

23 points

(Unit award 14 / 23)

Passage 4

Kein Appetit auf Fleisch

1. How long have Sarah and Laura been vegetarian?   **1 point**
    - since they were eleven

2. Why was this such a dramatic change for them?   **1 point**
    - they had been eating meat almost daily

3. What reason do they give for not liking meat?   **1 point**
    - they are disgusted at the thought
    OR
    - they find meat disgusting

4. Mention three negative aspects of the meat trade which might spoil your appetite.   **3 points**
    - mad cow disease
    - mass livestock farming
    - animal transportation scandals

5. What problematic food chain does the biology teacher mention?   **3 points**
    - many animals are fed antibiotics
    - humans then eat meat contaminated with antibiotics
    - antibiotics then become more ineffective in humans

6. What statistic are we given regarding the number of vegetarians at her school?   **1 point**
    - there is about one in every class

7. What reason is given for the high number of female vegetarians?   **2 points**
    - many girls say that they are fond of animals
    - they find slaughtering cruel / dreadful

8. What in particular prompted

    (a) Ümmihan   **1 point**
    - she experienced a ritual Moslem sacrifice

    (b) and Ines to give up eating meat?   **2 points**
    - she once saw a slaughtered cow hanging up
    - she was disgusted by the pools of blood
    - she realised what she was actually eating
      (any 2)

9. What effect do Ines and Denise think their vegetarianism will have on

    (a)   animals?   **1 point**
    - they will be helped

    (b)   the meat industry?   **1 point**
    - it will be damaged if more people follow their example

10. What point do Jennifer and Jenny make about most teenagers?   **1 point**
    - they do not think twice about eating hamburgers

11. Why did Yasmin give up meat?   **2 points**
    - her friend was giving it up for health reasons
    - she wanted to see if she could go without too

12. What did she have to do to compensate for the lack of protein in her new diet?   **1 point**
    - eat more fish and soya meat

13. What benefit has she noticed from her new, healthy diet?   **1 point**
    - she does not have weight problems

14. What does Lisa's mother have to buy for her daughter?   **1 point**
    - free-range eggs from the farmer

15. What final comment is made about domestic animals?   **1 point**
    - we would not want to slaughter and eat them

24 points

(Unit award 15 / 24)

Passage 5

Ein Ehrenamt

1. Why do Semir, Anne and the others think voluntary work is a good thing?   **2 points**
    - it is a lot of fun
    - you take on responsibility
    - you are given trust / you are trusted
      (any 2)

2. What exactly is Semir's job?   **1 point**
    - he trains the youngest members of a football club (with a co-trainer)

3. What does he particularly like about working with the boys?   **2 points**
    - their enthusiasm
    - they are never in a bad mood

4. How have his own skills improved in working with the boys?   **3 points**
    - he used to just run around (like an idiot)
    - he knows that you also need stretching exercises,
    - running and keep-fit exercises

5. What is their motto?   **1 point**
    - to always get on / along with each other

6. *(a)* Which hobby did Anne start over seven years ago?   **1 point**
    - singing in a school choir

    (b) Mention two tasks she now carries out.   **2 points**
    - she sometimes takes the rehearsals
    - she makes posters (on the computer) advertising their performances
    - she goes into shops and asks for the posters to be displayed / put up
      (any 2)

7. What is Arne doing in August?   **1 point**
    - he is travelling with 13–17 year old pupils to France

8. Mention two activities he and his friends are planning.   **2 points**
    - concerts
    - games
    - religious services
      (any 2)

9. Mention three things they have to see to.   **3 points**
                     • accommodation
                     • catering / meals
                     • first-aid kit
                     • the allocation of rooms
                     • washing-up rota
                     (any 3)

10. What does he find enjoyable on the trip itself?   **1 point**
                     • getting to know lots of people and different landscapes

11. What sort of work do Sabrina and Anna do?   **2 points**
                     • they coach a group of girls
                     • at their gymnastics club

12. Why do the trainers enjoy their time with the girls?   **3 points**
                     • the girls have far fewer worries / cares than the trainers
                     • when they tell them stories from their everyday lives the trainers
                       forget their own problems
                     • they trust the trainers / they place their trust in the trainers

24 points

(Unit award 15 / 24)

Passage 6

Traumberuf Schauspieler?

1. Who are the three people on the selection panel?   **3 points**
    - the producer
    - the production manager
    - the director

2. What do they have in a pile in front of them?   **2 points**
    - the actors' CVs
    - photographs of the actors

3. What are we told about the two characters?   **2 points**
    - they live in a shared flat / house
    - and have all kinds of problems with their neighbours

4. What is the first thing that is discussed with the actors?   **1 point**
    - how the producer and the director envisage the characters

5. What response do the actors get after their attempt at the first scene?   **2 points**
    - the director praises them
    - he explains how they could improve their interpretation of the role

6. After the filming, what are they asked to do?   **1 point**
    - to go into the next room and prepare for a reading of two minor
      parts

7. Once the casting team is alone again, what comments are made about the actor hoping to
    play Nils?   **1 point**
    - he is a very good actor

8. Why do they think he is not right for the part?   **2 points**
    - he is not tall enough to play Nils
    - he is not sporty enough
    - he is not the right type
      (any 2)

9. What do they not like about the actress?   **1 point**
    - her hair looks dreadful

10. What is the actress doing when her phone call comes?   **1 point**
       • she is preparing for another audition

11. *(a)* Why has this latest audition been particularly successful for her?   **2 points**
       • this is her first big part
       • after about 50 auditions

    (b) What other acting experience has she had?   **2 points**
       • she had a minor role as a cleaner
       • in a detective series

12. *(a)* Why is the actor not at home when he is called?   **1 point**
       • he is working as a waiter in a restaurant

    (b) What is he doing later with friends?   **1 point**
       • he is rehearsing a play for children

13. How does he respond to the message on his answering machine?   **2 points**
       • he is not bothered
      OR
       • he thinks it does not matter
      OR
       • he thinks he will be successful at the next audition
      OR
       • he is resolved to keep at it

24 points

(Unit award 15 / 24)

Passage 7

Im Rhythmus des Orients

1. (a) Why is it surprising to find the *Bodrum* dance floor full at 11pm?   **1 point**
        • it is still early for disco-goers

    (b) What is the most requested sort of music?   **1 point**
        • oriental-sounding music

    (c) Where exactly is the disco situated?   **2 points**
        • in the centre of Cologne
        • below a shoppping centre

2. (a) What existed on the site until a few months ago?   **1 point**
        • a poorly frequented pub / restaurant

    (b) Why do some of the original furnishings still exist?   **3 points**
        • the new owners did not want to take a risk
        • so they invested only in the most essential things
        • the *Bodrum* was only a trial project at first
        • no one knew if the idea would take off
        (any 3)

3. (a) According to Hussein Furol, what were young Turks missing in German discos?   **1 point**
        • Turkish music they had heard on their holidays in Turkey

    (b) What was his intention in opening the *Bodrum*?   **1 point**
        • he wanted to give them a place where they could hear their music
          and dance to it

4. (a) Why does Kemal like coming to the *Bodrum*?   **1 point**
        • because of the music the disco is for him both a part of Turkey
          and home

    (b) Why do Jashdan and Ipek often come to the *Bodrum*?   **3 points**
        • they know a lot of people there
        • it is a kind of youth centre where all the young people like to meet
        • the atmosphere is good
        • they feel at home there (they are happy there)
        (any 3)

5.   *(a)*   What happened to Ömer and Baçar at German discos?   **2 points**
- they were denied entry / had difficulty getting in
- the bouncers told them they were too badly dressed

    (b)   What evidence was there that this was racially motivated?   **1 point**
- the bouncers allowed entry to everyone else and they were dressed in exactly the same way

6.   What are we told about some of the more traditional Turkish girls in the disco?   **2 points**
- they are only allowed to come if they are with a brother or a cousin
- they are not allowed to dance with strangers / young men they do not know
- this is why there are lots of groups of girls on the dance floor (any 2)

7.   *(a)*   What plans are afoot for the *Bodrum*?   **2 points**
- the disco is to be extended
- a Turkish restaurant is to be opened

    (b)   What is Furol's wish for the future?   **2 points**
- more young Germans will come
- in nightlife the two cultures will one day mix

23 points

(Unit award 14 / 23)

Passage 8

In England herrscht nicht nur Nebel

1. What sort of school did Julius end up in? **1 point**
    - a boarding school

2. How does he contrast his activities with his classmates' in Germany? **2 points**
    - they were doing floor exercises
    - while he was playing rugby

3. *(a)* What comment does he make about the daily routine as a boarder? **1 point**
    - it is much more structured

    (b) Unlike in Germany, what does he have to get used to in England? **2 points**
    - not having to get up until 8 every day
    - staying longer in bed

4. What happened before the first period? **1 point**
    - the whole school attended assembly in the hall

5. What comment does he make about school lunch? **1 point**
    - it consisted mainly of British beef, potatoes and vegetables
    OR
    - it was quite tasty

6. Mention three things he says about cricket. **3 points**
    - a match lasts five days
    - when you had a lot of work it was a good way to relax
    - it is no fun when it rains

7. What happened between 7 and 9 pm? **1 point**
    - they did their homework in their rooms

8. In what way did the boarders break the school rules? **1 point**
    - they went to the pub

9. Why were they unlikely to get drunk? **2 points**
    - there was little time
    - the houses / halls were locked at 10 pm / they had to be back by 10 pm

10. What was the punishment if caught?   **1 point**
  • expulsion / you had to leave the school / you had to pack your things

11. What information are we given about one third of the boarders?   **1 point**
  • they did not come from the UK

12. Where did Julius make many of his friends?   **2 points**
  • in a drama group
  • as captain of the football team

13. What decision did he make?   **2 points**
  • to stay on for a second year
  • to sit his final school exams in England

14. What is Julius doing now?   **1 point**
  • he is studying economics in London

15. What comment does he make about the attitude of the English towards the Germans?   **1 point**
  • a lot of prejudice exists towards the Germans

16. What does he say about the English weather?   **1 point**
  • it is not as bad as you think

                                                                                          24 points

                                                                                 (Unit award 15 / 24)

Passage 9

Tokyo am Rhein

1. Mention two things you might be surprised to find in the middle of Düsseldorf. **2 points**
   - Japanese shops and restaurants
   - a temple and a Japanese garden

2. *(a)* Why was Yuuki delighted to move to Germany? **1 point**
   - he was about to sit an important and difficult exam at his school

   (b) What does he say about Japanese schools? **1 point**
   - the pressure is much greater

   (c) What are the lessons like in his school in Düsseldorf? **2 points**
   - they are taught in English
   - they also learn German and Japanese
   - the pupils are all Japanese
   (any 2)

3. What is the difference between school meals and mealtimes at home? **3 points**
   - at school the food is traditionally German
   - at home they eat Japanese meals – a lot of rice, vegetables and fish
   - they use chopsticks at home

4. *(a)* What does Mai particularly value in Germany? **1 point**
   - she values nature / the countryside

   (b) What does she say about families in Japan? **1 point**
   - they rarely go for walks in the country

   (c) What information are we given about shopping in Japan? **2 points**
   - the shops are open 24 hours
   - many Japanese use the weekend to go shopping

5. What is Yuuki's new hobby? **1 point**
   - he plays billiards

6. What would Japanese young people much rather do? **1 point**
   - play computer games

7. Which Japanese custom is carried out at Yuuki's house?   **2 points**
> • visitors are asked to remove their shoes
> • at the front door / before coming in

8. What can his homepage be used for?   **2 points**
> • to find out about Germany in English or Japanese
> • e.g. the confusing Düsseldorf tram and underground charges / fares

9. What will happen in two years?   **1 point**
> • their fathers' stay in Germany will come to an end

10. What will the two young people have achieved by then?   **1 point**
> • they will have their school leaving certificate

11. What are their plans for the future at the moment?   **2 points**
> • they may move away from their parents
> • Mai is looking forward to returning to Japan
> • Yuuki envisages studying and living somewhere else
> (any 2)

23 points

(Unit award 14 / 23)

RECORD OF ACHIEVEMENT   Student Name ....

The following can be used to record your marks and will help you to monitor your own progress.

READING

Lifestyles	Questions (20)	Translation (10)	Total Mark (30)
Passage 1			
Passage 2			
Passage 3			
Passage 4			
Passage 5			

Education & Work	Questions (20)	Translation (10)	Total Mark (30)
Passage 6			
Passage 7			
Passage 8			
Passage 9			
Passage 10			

The Wider World	Questions (20)	Translation (10)	Total Mark (30)
Passage 11			
Passage 12			
Passage 13			

DIRECTED WRITING

	Mark out of 15		Mark out of 15
Directed Writing 1		Directed Writing 6	
Directed Writing 2		Directed Writing 7	
Directed Writing 3		Directed Writing 8	
Directed Writing 4		Directed Writing 9	
Directed Writing 5		Directed Writing 10	

END OF UNIT READING

Lifestyles	mark	unit award	pass/fail
Passage 1	/ 24	15 / 24	
Passage 2	/ 23	14 / 23	
Passage 3	/ 23	14 / 23	
Passage 4	/ 24	15 / 24	
Education & Work			
Passage 5	/ 24	15 / 24	
Passage 6	/ 24	15 / 24	
The Wider World			
Passage 7	/ 23	14 / 23	
Passage 8	/ 24	15 / 24	
Passage 9	/ 23	14 / 23	